5/93

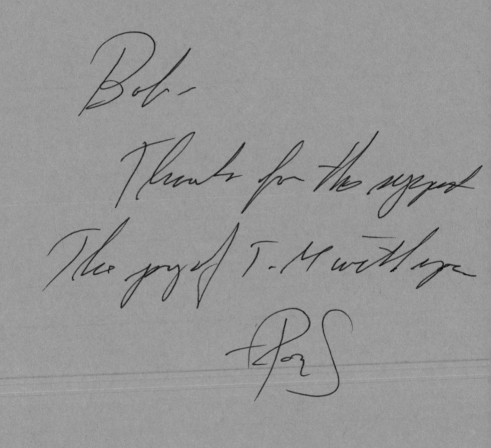

Bob -

Thanks for the support

The joy of T-M with age

P.S.

Song for Nobody

Meditation seat in the woods of the monastery, Abbey of Gethsemani, Trappist, Kentucky.

Song for Nobody

A Memory Vision of
Thomas Merton

Ron Seitz

Triumph™ Books
Liguori, Missouri

Photographs

Abbey of Gethsemani Archives–pages: 18, 40, 48, 54
John Howard Griffin–page 27
John Hutchison–pages: 175, 182–183
Thomas Merton–pages: 58, 71, 157, 187
Ron Seitz–pages: 2, 26, 42, 65, 66, 83, 84, 87, 89, 105, 117, 118, 121, 132,
    133, 136, 156, 177, 180

Published by Triumph™ Books
Liguori, Missouri
An Imprint of Liguori Publications

Library of Congress Cataloging-in-Publication Data

Seitz, Ron
      Song for nobody : a memory vision of Thomas Merton / Ron Seitz. —
1st ed.
          p.   cm.
      ISBN 0-89243-486-4 : $19.95
      1. Merton, Thomas, 1915–1968.   2. Trappists — United States–
  –Biography.   I. Title.
BX4705.M542S45   1993
271' .12502 — dc20
[B]
                                                                    92-43419
                                                                         CIP

Copyright© 1993 by Ron Seitz
Printed in the United States of America
First Edition

with deep love and gratitude
this book
is dedicated to
my wife
Sally

Books by Ron Seitz

Requiem

The Gethsemani Poems

Death Eat

Monks Pond. Old Hermit. Hai!

Cables Across the Ohio

Poet Pray

The Mechanic of Tears

Being Center

Acknowledgments

Portions of this book have appeared in the following publications: *The Courier-Journal Magazine, High Roads Folio, Kentucky Poetry Review, Larkspur Press, The Merton Seasonal, U.S. Catholic, Way.*

The author wishes to thank the Robert Lee Blaffer Trust and the George W. Norton Foundation, without whose support this book would not have been possible.

Special appreciation is extended to Abbot Timothy Kelly, Brother Patrick Hart, Jane Norton, Jane Owen, Doug Stegner, Nana Lampton, Robert Daggy, Tommie O' Callaghan, Dr. William P. VonderHarr, and all the monks at the Abbey of Gethsemani . . . whose friendship and encouragement gave me the will and the time to complete this work.

Finally, I would like to thank my editor, Pat Kossmann, whose patience and professionalism helped bring this book into being.

Contents

Song for Nobody

A yellow flower
(Light and spirit)
Sings by itself
For nobody.

A golden spirit
(Light and emptiness)
Sings without a word
By itself.

Let no one touch this gentle sun
In whose dark eye
Someone is awake.

(No light, no gold, no name, no color
And no thought:
O, wide awake!)

A golden heaven
Sings by itself
A song to nobody.

Thomas Merton

Foreword

MOST COMMENTATORS TO DATE on the life and thought of Thomas Merton — and they are legion — have been writers and scholars of various disciplines, who have approached the poet monk from their own particular backgrounds and interests. They have provided valuable insights into the paradoxical character of one of the most extraordinary monks of all times, and have in their assessment of his achievement made obvious his enormous legacy to the past, present, and future. A smaller number were Merton's poet friends such as Robert Lax, Mark Van Doren, Sister Thérèse Lentfoehr, Ernesto Cardenal, Raïssa Maritain, Brother Antoninus, and Daniel Berrigan, to name only a few. To this latter group must be added Ron Seitz, who not only knew Merton well, but was also a poet/friend and confidante, able to identify with many of the monk's interests and enthusiasms.

It has taken Seitz a long time to document his special relationship with Merton, but now in time for the twenty-fifth anniversary of Merton's passage through death to life, we finally have the engaging account of a unique relationship, a remembrance portrait like none other. Merton comes alive in Seitz's account of their friendship over the years. It was a non-judgmental love, one that allowed the other to be other, always respecting the space of the friend and the way the Spirit led on life's journey. Seitz's own monastic dimension is obvious throughout the narrative. Only one who intuitively grasps the essence of the monastic quest can write as he does.

That is why I can say without hesitation that at last here is the Merton I knew. The reason, I believe, is that the author is himself essentially a poet with a profound understanding of the monastic charism, one who has entered into the master/disciple relationship rather than simply a detached observer standing on the outside trying to make Merton fit into some preconceived idea.

On behalf of many monks and numerous friends who knew Merton during his lifetime, I want to thank Ron Seitz for his sharing of a very intimate friendship in *Song for Nobody*, and for all the "blood, sweat, and tears" that went into writing this fascinating memoir. In poetry and prose, the author has given us a very readable, well-written portrait of Thomas Merton — the very alive human being whom most people would like to meet.

Brother Patrick Hart, O.C.S.O.
Abbey of Gethsemani

Let me tell you of Tom Merton . . . in my waking reveries, my memoried visions of a phantom passing-thru of someone I loved and now so miss.

Tom Merton — the monk and man who was my life double, the shade of my hulk amove in time for some ten years while alive, and now twenty more winters in death.

A ghost of a dream, a shadow cast forward to envelope my spirit. A spectre cloak to wrangle my weight upon the pavement, to block my free flow fall. The echoed tome that will not still the tomb. The heavy gravemark I carry aback all these days, so weary with write . . . .

And lay down here this imaged person.
To rest in peace, the call complete.

Part One

In the beginning . . .

MIDNIGHT, DECEMBER 17, 1968—
NOON, DECEMBER 18, 1968

IT IS ALMOST MIDNIGHT NOW and I am in my small writing cell in the basement—really an old coal bin emptied and swept out, with mixtures of odd, leftover paint whitewashing the walls. Sally has just perked a fresh pot of coffee and brought that good, dark brew-smell from the kitchen down here to warm and wake up the place.

It is blessed and peaceful this way, with the entire house silent and asleep, and the wide clean pages of the notebook ready for the first words to loop and roll along the lines. And I'm ready to try again my secret scribble for a few hours—hopefully till dawn lights the small window above my desk and puts its signature to this say.

I have my hunting boots and thick, hooded sweater on, but, just as out at the hermitage, it is cold in this unheated room. Head bent to the page and eyes peeping out of the wool cowl, I keep rubbing my hands, wrapping them around the hot coffee mug after each few lines scrawled.

The other side of this concrete wall the temperature is down to eight degrees. A beautiful night, with just the beginning of snow

15

flurries blowing out there. Good to write into the deepening hours, feeling one with the bare black tree in the yard just ten feet away.

That lone tree in the dark, its limbs heavy with waiting for the snow-filled sky to come, open, and cover everything with white, deep by dawn — ready for the first prints of my stepping out of this write-long reverie, this memory portrait, finally spent of language. In this first shock and numbness and disbelief in what has happened — Tom gone now, and forever.

But . . . where to begin, and how? There's so much left unsaid and no particular order to the putting down of these thoughts, impressions, visions.

Even as I write here now, I am wrapped in and ride the windy cold bell echoes of late afternoon Vespers gathering the night, folding in with gray the whole stone structure of the faraway Abbey church with ghost steeple pointing silver to the sky cloud-moving, darkening. The December look of it that made me want to forever walk those shadowed hallways with head bowed, arms enfolded in my heavy wool habit.

God! In my simple naive innocence I wanted that hungry hollow-cheek pale feel and look, that clean-bone purity of a monk in solitude. The silence.

Tom Merton — Could he ever have known who he was to me then . . . our first meeting?

———————————◆———————————

I was a college boy, fresh out of the Army. And by some chance — or crooked line of Providence — I found (or was handed) his books. First the poems: all of those nature images blooming the Gethsemani landscape, those beautiful evocative hymns singing holy their prayer-praise to God in a monk's makeshift lyrical liturgy enclosed by no church other than the wide domed sky arching high over the whole monastery altar.

Then, young in spirit as never before or since, my huge innocent appetite was fed by the vision of *The Seven Storey Mountain.* As many of my generation — young men of the 50s, a nomadic community of social and artistic rebels, rejecting our culture for spiritual reasons — I now sought out the same monastery gate, wanting to pound my fists on the heavy wooden door of Gethsemani, wanting to touch what was breathing behind those moss-covered enclosure walls: the imaginary cells of solitude and silence that would beckon us, also, to the monk's cowl. Tom's voice an ascetic song to heaven, his autobiography a testament that we so wanted to be ours, his story a journey much like our own.

Tom Merton — Could he have ever known what he was doing with his words, his vision, his presence! I not knowing then that he was only some fifty miles away from me in Louisville. So close, speaking his person into writing.

No Man Is an Island, Seeds of Contemplation — those 'little' paperback books curled close in the palm of my hand, stuffed snug in my back pocket wherever I went those days. Small pages of private meditations to be read alone, in silence. To send me reading the Christian mystics: St. John of the Cross and Teresa of Avila.

I even had my own rock-quarry hermitage near my home (really a nook beneath a brambled overhang) where I lit stick fires and meditated, writing little snow poems, winter haiku

> white and cold, alone
> it slants fast into the grass—
> the first flake of snow

It was there, in that makeshift cell, that I read Tom's *Sign of Jonas.* The Trappist woods were never so alive as then. Or now.

"Dear God — *this*, this only, is enough!" I used to say aloud. "I don't need or ask for anything else."

So young and innocent and 'believing' then — I was *moved*. Moved as I think I will never be again. Because I was 'open' to beauty and grace . . . my Spirit vulnerable. I felt the stirring in my blood, the pulse and urge to 'touch' what was breathing inside those books. Tom's voice: an icy finger that ran quick through my chestcage, that pierced the heart, to touch the sleeping soul of me. To seek out that monastery hid (welcome) somewhere in the woods of Trappist, Kentucky. Yes, sought out the cold stone arched *pax intrantibus* of Gethsemani's gate. Eyes, arms, and palms open to embrace the cold iron crosses of the Abbey cemetery — my one final, true home.

A long way from then to now, from there to here. From that bright light to this dark shadow.

Have been at this for almost an hour now, scribbling these journal notes. My hands are cramped. Looking back over these few pages, I can hardly decipher my scrawl. So hurried and sloppy the

"Peace to those entering." Gatehouse of Gethsemani Abbey grounds.

writing's become as I rush to get it all down before the dawn deadline. —All? impossible. —Deadline? what reason?

Must stop a moment. Collect myself.

Step outside for a breath of air. Rest empty.

•

My brief retreat to the waking cold of the sideyard was interrupted. Again, the phone. More of the same as a week ago, Tuesday, the day of Tom's death, when at midnight a young local poet called and wanted to know, "What's it all about?" — having just picked up an early edition of the paper to read the "unbelievable news." He wanted to talk, to have company in his own grief and loss then. But I had been through so much that day already and was so wrung-out, exhausted, that I just wanted to get back to bed and would talk to him later. Inconsiderate and uncharitable, I know. But for those first twelve hours Tom's death numbed me, dumbed me. So much so that I just walked around waiting for something revelatory to happen, whether to me or the world it didn't matter. Waiting for the big change inside of me that would set things right so I would be whole again. Saying to myself:

Thomas Merton is dead. December 10, 1968. In Bangkok.
How strange, so far from home, Kentucky. Gethsemani.
A monk in his hut. Poet in a monastery. Friend to us all.

What are we to do now — those whom he touched?

Jerked away clean by death, he left a hole in our lives.
There's emptiness now in the world.
One of the strings (the two or three good men who hold up the world)
    has been broken.
And, left wronged by the loss, which of us will right it?

Let it be known, Tom Merton — you were a POET.
A poet, first and always.
No philosopher, theologian, social crusader.

You sang your presence in poetry. Breathed beauty into our lives.
You gathered us all in, put a pulse to our innocence, locked love
    in our hearts.

Then left. Fled smiling, still singing. Parting the trees and waters
    with laughter.
A joyous time of it, you had.

And we are deeper, more true, for your going.
We have been called to task.
Yours, the note let loose. Ours, the word unsaid.

Do we hear? And will we answer?
That is our calling.

A thousand years, a thousand poems, will not undo you, Thomas Merton.

You are whole.
Make us so.

And just now, a week later, remembering all this, I finally cried. A deep hurt and loss and emptiness inside. Feeling now the big hole that is in my life. Realizing now just how much a part of me Tom was.

And that's how it is: *Tom's presence always there* (presence in the true sense of the word, *person*), and I not knowing just how real it was.

To give you an idea of how wrought and twisted emotionally, how disorientated I had become those first few days after Tom's death — on a sudden impulse of guilt and unworthiness in the light of my living and he being dead, I took an electric razor and shaved my head as an act of purgation, a cleansing of my terminal vanity.

So, you see, the past week just slid by as if a half dream, hazy and dulled. And I'm just now somewhat coming out of it (by the mere act of writing this). We've got to go on, those of us left here behind. That's all there is to it. Because no matter how much poorer we may be or how different things are now that Tom's gone, there's little choice in the matter, eh?

Why I am here now, the middle of the night, talking to you with pen and paper. Because I had the rare opportunity and blessed privilege to spend so much time with Tom Merton his last ten years here in Kentucky, especially those months before he made his departure for the East, his (as it so sadly turned out) 'final leave-taking.'

And so many memories that fill me now. . . .

———◆———

Memories—
Of the frequent trips I've made down to the monastery the past twelve years. Whether for a retreat or just a visit, I would always attend the prayer services. Especially *Vigils* at three o'clock in the morning . . . a dazed euphoria at the holiness of such an hour.

There, in the dark balcony, the high-walled length of the church before me, I would peer down at the heads and half-hid faces of the monks as their voices rose and fell in Gregorian chant floating the cold air. I was going to catch a glimpse of Thomas Merton, hoping to recognize the 'Holy Monk' from my memory of one of those early photographs that had appeared somewhere— that young bald head and expressionless face. *Expressionless,*

I thought, because already emptied of worldly desires and hang-ups and anxious doubts.

So untrue, I now know. But then . . . so full of open-mouthed need and hope, I wanted and prayed to know that there was *something somewhere* still good and untainted by all of the vulgarity and noise that cluttered my own soul. —What I sought in the person of Tom Merton.

Yes, looking for the face of young Tom, the one I found in his *Secular Journal*. The 'promising' young writer high on mountains and wine, the jazz-pianist author of several novels that he later burned upon entering the monastery . . . how noble and coura-geous and dedicated and saintly to do this, I thought. —The confi-dent swagger, bravado farewell salute to literature.

Tom Merton . . . the once brash self-named 'Communist'. Fresh out of Columbia and on to Bonaventure, making his pilgrimage to Cuba.

All this between beer-drinking sessions in a New York tavern with his professor-friend, Dan Walsh. The two of them intimately considering Tom's conversion, his possible future vocation as a poet, priest, monk, contemplative at the Abbey of Gethsemani in Kentucky. Tom discussing philosophy and theology with short stout prizefighter-looking, good Dr. Dan.

Dan Walsh — who would, in his last years, leave Columbia and New York City and move here to Kentucky to be near the person he loved most on this planet, to live at the Abbey and in Louisville, to teach the monks the dawn mysteries of medieval truth — to teach me too at Bellarmine College, where I was an 'unknowing Prof' carrying messages back and forth between the two of them.

Good wise Dan. The instrument of my personal relationship with Thomas Merton for over ten years. Dan Walsh — finally, sixty years old (and a *priest* all along, but not 'officially'), he decided to put on the black and the Roman collar, and happy, verily, to say Mass.

I remember Tom smiling at the thought of Dan becoming a priest. Tom called Dan a 'dreamer'; Dan called Tom a 'dreamer'. Each saying this to me (privately) in loving admiration of the other. And when I read Tom's books, I would hear Dan's words; when I heard Dan's voice, I would see Tom's words. —From whom first these truths? Neither. Both.

But the joy of being in their presence — an experience of revelation. My head and heart a huge dry wheatfield set aflame each
time I entered into this blessed 'teaching'. —Dan carrying secret
messages from the monastery ("Tom says . . .") and Tom announcing holy mysteries from Dan got.

This man (old in body, young in spirit), soft-spoken, humble,
saintly even — and me brash, eager, ignorant in my prolonged youth
and vanity. Nevertheless, Dan sometimes proud of me to Tom, and
other times (I know) embarrassed. His highest praise and compliment to me one day after a long talk: "Ron, I think that you are
undergoing a true conversion." —Meaning so much to me because
he had been the instrument of (present at, a catalyst in) Tom's spiritual birth. I trusted that he knew what he was talking about!

What I'm coming to here, and briefly, is another remembered
moment (maybe the best one) that Tom and I shared with Dan
Walsh: his Ordination, First Mass. . . . No, it will take another, better
than myself, to re-create in words the 'mystery' of that sacred event.

After that special Mass, there was a reception at the home of
Tommie O'Callaghan, a close friend to all of us. It was a cloudy
afternoon, with Tom and the Abbot present (a day's leave from the
monastery into the city) to concelebrate the service, then afterwards to celebrate socially the occasion of this happy event with
good friends and food and drinks.

The incident forever framed in my memory of that day is of
Tom Merton, somewhat uncomfortable in the large living room,
surrounded by a growing group of well-meaning admirers (all curious). Tom was being asked a wide variety of sincere questions
(mostly of an ecclesiastical nature). And listening patiently, from
time to time refilling his champagne glass and sipping it ever more
rapidly to sustain his kind attention, he finally spread his arms as a
gentle gesture of calling a halt to all of this, with: "Okay, okay, let's
hold a moment . . . this is all fine and good, but the real issue here
is whether or not *God is in this room, here and now!*" Pausing, with
arms still spread, a smile widening to a cheerful grin, eyes open
with light (everyone caught, still, silenced with listening), "If you
are in the truth of that — then all of these other concerns take care
of themselves, eh?

"Sure."

And with that, Tom had graciously backed out of the crowded
room with the neck of the large champagne bottle in one hand and

an empty glass in the other. Through the wide door and outside onto the brick patio, taking a deep breath of fresh air, he walked past several clusters of people, nodding hello politely, and headed straight towards my wife Sally . . . just as the sun broke thru the clouds to light up the open yard a few brief moments.

And that's my single, best-remembered image of Tom that day: dressed formally (for a monk) in his black suit and Roman collar, sitting at a small, white lawn table in the garden in the sun with Sally all glowing happy in her pale yellow chiffon dress and matching wide straw hat — each of them more beautiful for being together, in relaxed talk and joyous laughter, toasting the day and Dan with raised glasses sparkling with that bubbly, cool white wine. And as I walked up to join them that sunny afternoon, I heard Tom's immortal definition and appreciation of the poet's beverage, "Champagne's no good unless you drink it all!"

And's true. We did just that.

A bright spot there to scatter the shadow of what I'm about here now — trying to write my way through the grief, a love-weep of loss. But that flower of a winter not the complete role of Dan Walsh in this memory vision.

About three o'clock of that deathday, last Tuesday, right after my final class, I came into the college lobby and Dan walked up to me (his eyes bloodshot from crying) and said, "Ron, I've got bad news. I hate to tell you this. Brace yourself for a shock."

And here I was weak, thinking that something must have happened to one of my sons, because I had just overheard Dan telling the switchboard operator that, "He must have fallen across a wire fence and electrocuted himself." —And I didn't know who he was talking about when he turned to me and said, "Tom's dead."

The words did not die on the air, but just hung frozen between our eyes, solid — as if etched in marble on a headstone. Everything just stopped inside me, held for a moment . . . then crumbled. I didn't cry. I didn't say anything. What had been whole in me was broken. Just as Dan had said later, that same night, as we sat in my car parked atop the hill overlooking the college. It was raining hard, splattering against the windshield, and Dan was crying unashamedly, "It's like I've been split down the middle. Like someone took half of me away. He was part of me . . . I don't think I can ever be the same again."

And Dan was there again last night, just a week later, after the Abbey funeral Mass and Tom's burial, at the seven o'clock special service at St. Agnes Church here in Louisville — a memorial to Merton that included prayers, songs, eulogies, and readings by friends and followers of the good monk. Dan was seated in the front pew with several other persons who had been very close to Tom for many more years than I knew him — among them John Howard Griffin (later, Tom's biographer), Naomi Burton (Tom's life-long literary advisor), and too many others to name here. I mention John Howard and Naomi especially because they were well-known and much better writers than the shaved head who was about to open his mouth and read:

> 2 poems dear Tom & high again
>
> time it is spill my say
> walk the wire of song barking my eyes
> all those weeps & childy dreams
> lost flaming along the pavement
>
> forgive me the knuckles upon your door
> old Poet
> I don't have a rose to wield
> cheeks to ring this day
>
> but I do know the sting of your beauty
> & must kiss you some way

My favorite poem to Tom. Embarrassed reading it then, and even now (the typed copy scotch-taped to the wall in front of me as I write).

I remember handing him that poem about eight months ago and watching him read it. How insensitive of me (and uncomfortable for him) to do that, but I wanted so much to tell him what my poems were trying to say indirectly with the inadequate equipment of language. Ever since our first meeting, I had been feeding him my writing, and so many of my poems over the years had been written *directly to him.*

That was the case when he asked for some material to publish in his literary magazine *Monks Pond* this past year and I gave him a large stack of poems. A week later, when we met again out at his hermitage, Tom said, "Ron, hey these poems are real good and all, but I can't publish stuff about me in my own magazine. Oh, I agree with you here (laughing), but it just wouldn't look right, eh."

But, you see, Tom Merton was not only my spiritual father — he was my mentor as well. And when he told me that same day at the hermitage (after looking at many other pieces, several of which he would later publish in *Monks Pond*), "You're a damned good poet, Ron!" . . . That's all I needed to encourage and sustain me in this most lonely and anonymous undertaking, *writing*. And writing not as 'literature', but as a form of *prayer*! —And always my poetry (my praying) to be heard by him as I did it.

It's strange (and Tom probably never knowing) how, when writing, I imagined my 'audience of one' to be him more than myself. —And I think that this will always be somewhat the case, if I have the grace and courage to continue.

—What I am about here, again, this morning . . . with words, my only way.

———◆———

As I look up to the side of me, on the wood shelf above my desk, I see a photograph of Tom. The snapshot — quick, unposed, natural—that someone (Bob Lax? myself?) took last spring at one of our picnics out at the monastery near Monks Pond. Good picture! But, when shown to him later, Tom remarked, "Dear God! if it's come to that, I'm finished."

Why his embarrassed response? Because the photo shows him grinning, with some strange secret mirth behind his eyes. A baseball cap cocked jauntily on the back of his head, leaning atilt in his chair against the stone block monastery wall. In that picture, possibly the *real* Thomas Merton: caught frozen, looking into the camera squint-eyed ("come on now"), a cat smile curling his mouth and pushing his cheeks high and shining — displaying again, in his ever-present shyness, that clean smooth look of healthy youth.

Why Tom didn't particularly like this photo — or at least said he didn't — I don't know. Unless, it caught him as he truly was and too modest to show: basically, a quite 'simple and ordinary' person. Maybe even appearing somewhat naive in his innocence. Ah, that's it! Found out! —A 'playful boy', that's who. The *innocent*: one who is full of awe and wonder at 'the first time Gift of everything in Creation'. Really that, always that, and nothing more.

Thomas Merton against the monastery wall, Abbey of Gethsemani.

What I told a newspaper reporter two nights after Tom's death, "Print this, if anything. —Merton was first of all *young!* . . . in the sense of being a poet. . . then that philosopher-theologian bit, or any highbrow scholarly commentator on ideas and books. But, at the heart — just a plain ol' poet singing it with joy and laughter."

Young, yes. And laughing, always.

Tom, the great laugher. God, was he ever that! —Open-mouthed "Oh Ah Ha" with head thrown back, hands on hips. The image that hangs afloat in my memory now as I see him standing back there at Monks Pond: Tom, after glancing at his photo-grin, laughing, "Got me! Up against the monastery wall, you mobster monk!"

Looping his thumbs over the black leather belt pulled tight across his stomach beginning to round into a paunch, "I'm getting fat from the easy life out here in the woods eating and sleeping and having too many picnics with all that good food that lovely Sally cooks up and you bring down with cold beer too . . . it's too much!"

A joke, of course. He knew, I knew. That kind of get-together rare and in marked contrast to the austere and disciplined life he was leading as a hermit in his last few years. The hermitage, far from being an escape from the world, had become for him a place to share in the struggles and sufferings of all those others, like myself, on the 'outside'.

—And he could do this best through the life of silence and solitude founded in monastic vows.

Oh, but Tom's laughter was open and honest and spontaneous: what was so refreshing about him, what made his face light up, his eyes actually twinkle. What I thought only happened in fairy tales. Maybe so. —It just might be that we had one going there for us . . . before Death stepped in like rain on that last of our open picnics under the sky out in those Gethsemani woods.

And that is how I want best to remember Thomas Merton — a little pudgy in his too-big, baggy overalls, with workshirt unbuttoned a few loops at the neck. Standing there with legs spread, grinning, one hand on hip, the other raised in an open palm wave, "Goodbye-Hello" . . . what matter? both the same, coming or going, *always there*!

Oh, he's that other guy too — the one I see in the stark light-and-shadow John Howard Griffin portrait framed on my desk in front of me now as I write. That's good. A face silent and pensive and peaceful. An expression looking even (God forbid) a little 'saintly'. An image that Tom didn't want and wouldn't like — what

Fr. Louis Merton.

with so many years having to contend with such. All of those 'pious religious' people (well-intentioned, true; having read his books too) thinking Thomas Merton the holy card figure, pale and ascetic-looking, gaunt lean from fasting, eyes perpetually heavenward, feet not quite touching the ground. The many times when he was hospitalized in Louisville, and those good humble people knocking on the door and sneaking quietly into his room to pay homage (myself included), really sometimes almost ready to kiss his robe or sandals. The kind of thing that made Tom want to close his door to the 'outside world' — but didn't, and never would.

The sound of something ticking the window pane above my desk wakes me from my stare at Tom's photograph. Thin shadows jerking the other side of the glass. The wind. A haiku

> so cold out there and
> something in the dark to fear—
> winter scratch of weeds

Things glaze over and come together in a rush the middle of the night. I sit here trying to get down on paper a few remembrances of what it was to have touched Tom in our passing-thru. All of the things not mentioned. But I am too exhausted (physically and emotionally) to go on with this (having switched to the typewriter hours ago).

Maybe later, twenty years from now, when the present pain has died away and I am more at peace with myself and Tom being gone. Then, when (and if) that time comes, recall and write in detail some of those moments we shared. —What I said I was going to do (but never did) in the letter I wrote him (but never mailed) right after he left that last time.

Dear Tom,

To begin, I realize that these random scattered idea-notes, inspired poem-jottings, this (sometimes) ecstatic testimony, testament really — none of it is 'orderly', not always coherent, hardly 'intelligible'. Nor will be the many words words to pages pages that will continue this Open Journal Monk Say to a friend and fellow pilgrim with what number of Ps etched on our foreheads as together we go the Storey Climb to Heaven.

What I'm saying, Tom, is that time just might run out on me this 'passing-thru' and I won't have the opportunity to clean this Message up! No honeyed esthete leisure to 're-work and edit' these holy motes of language to avoid repetition, discard a sloppy muse, or abort whatever meandering 'blind' this frenzied pulse leads me.

Because there is a spell upon and over me, a drive — almost a 'chant compulsion (Rilkean angel-trumpeteer) to Say' what I write here. And speak it Now . . . keep going till the flow cease.

So forgive me this fiery urge to cable you my Spiritual Conversion, my dying to the world in order to Live the World! —I've got to get it down fast.

Maybe later, if worthwhile, someone who's on the same wave and 'appreciates' this scribble can 'purge the clutter' and make something of it for others. But right now, I'm just not up to that and must continue to scrawl this script till I Burn Up With Beauty!

Enough, Tom, enough! My head a-hurrying, my mind a brushfire. Thoughts, images — a run-on endless heart movie I can hardly control. Everything I read, everything I see, everyone I touch, lights me up — I come shining Alive!

Love to you . . . and all. —Here goes.

Just another piece of yellowing paper stuck to the wall in front of me, the dry corners curling, as I lean close to read the dead words.

The bottom of the window is piling with snow . . .

> I sit awake
> watching the world
> fill up with snow

the only light the white
on limbs covered
waving

white white
the trees move
in the snowing

I am alone
waiting empty
on this dark page

a winter night
out there the other side
of the window

the Monk is moving

It will soon be dawn. The limbs will reach their fingers to snow
come five o'clock — a welcome.
To continue this? Maybe.
But first, a few hours sleep, something to eat—
Then . . . .

———————◆———————

Earth's a good place to die from.
Woke after two hours sleep with these words on my lips. As
every night since Tom's death, I have dreamed of him again. And
before getting out of bed I wrote down the dream as quickly as
possible in my night journal, before it faded. But because so very
intense, I was unable to capture totally the memory of it and doubt
that I can communicate it to anyone. What follows is but a general
outline with somewhat vague details, exactly as I jotted it down
upon waking . . . one of my most beautiful experiences:

*Tom is standing at the edge of a dirt road and I am on the other side.
The lay of the land slants down away from Tom's feet, rounding to a
horizon.*
*Tom looks to me, then points his extended arm in about a forty-five
degree angle to the sky of the horizon. And I, looking over his head in
that direction, see a crooked broken line of birds flying in some sort of V*

formation. They are flying, passing left to right, out away from us maybe one hundred yards.

And Tom says: "See. See those birds!"

And I look up to see the birds and they are moving slowly, floating (no wing flap) . . . and the edges of their wings all around on both sides are thinly transparent, really translucent! — the 'see-through' light a pulse of aura-breath to me.

The birds are moving so fluidly, afloat, total ease, and the formation a slow waver, shifting shape in a sway-lift, then down-tilt, the end birds swinging up then back ever so 'softly'. . . the formation all of a piece though, one group of many birds.

And then Tom says: "See those birds . . . the way they are moving, their motion . . . that is the Love that moves Creation!"

What he seemed to be saying to me in 'communion', and what I grasped immediately (much more than his words merely intimated) — that flying, fluid, free movement of Life immanent with the Light of Love (God the Creator) is the *imaged music* of the Divine Will . . . that harmony of motion is the mystical expression (as best I can *show* you) of Divine Presence in Creation — Revelation!

While here, two other dreams, both during the night following Tom's death. These more brief because not written down, so entirely from memory. The first:

While talking to Tom I see his face, then entire head become a glowing sphere of almost blinding white light. And without actually speaking, he says to me:

"This is who I really am . . . if you are seeking to find out, to know me."

His so-called 'individual identity' was negated, displaced, 'gone', and replaced (what was never really there anyway) by this *other*, manifest as *light!*

The second dream:

Again I am looking at Tom, possibly talking to him, and then suddenly his head becomes 'transparent' (no! that's not the right word — because I can more than just see through his head to what lies immediately the other side of him).

The experience is that I look through his head as an 'open see' to the BEYOND, which is actually 'telescoped' or directed to his beginning/his existence origin, a specific place and climate of time from whence he came as human — as if he is saying to me:

"If you want to know how I came to be the man I am, what brought me to this place as the person named Thomas Merton — this earthly point is where I entered, began the journey, the life-trip."

And that telescoped view through which I look, his 'transparent viewfinder' head, narrows to a specific place somewhere in the East.

In these dreams Tom and I had been talking, moving, all the time both of us knowing, having discussed it — the fact that Tom is dead and I am alive. And . . . this situation not really surprising or a concern to either of us.

Enough about the dreams for now.

While eating breakfast (some cheese, toast, and coffee) I kept thinking of Tom — about what a 'strange' one he was, strange in the sense of his ordinary way of being. I thought of him as a 'naturalborn hound' with nose nuzzling the ground, hot to the scent of the breathing body: Life! . . . the supreme miracle of just being here—and someone else too! . . . *Find that other and touch with love!*

I had watched him move along that long crooked line of God, passing through his young dance of skepticism with energetic buoyancy, soon deflated to cynicism (the agnostic) and out again — esthetics his escape to religiosity that deepened to the spiritual by way of asceticism, and going . . . going on to what? — I don't know.

But *going!* Fluid, river-winding, around-the-next-bend, in the dark. But *joyous* (always) with 'expectation' and surprise. Welcoming 'open-souled' — without check, reservations, qualifications, no fear of who he was — a wide-mouthed gulping of the 'mystery unknown'.

And surprising to some, I had always held on to the 'living company of his presence' across that stretch of land between my cell here in Louisville to his home some fifty miles away at the monastery, Gethsemani. Even now I am acutely conscious of, and in 'spiritual touch' with him. There was always my *comfort-knowing* of Tom being out in that hermitage, and I enjoyed his 'loving company' even though not seeing or being with him in person.

And even moreso now, with the distance of death between us, I know that Tom continues his life of silence, of solitude (made total, pure, in eternity) — forever the contemplative, the mystic . . . the flow continuing to grow, branching in whatever direction his soul freely moves him. —But, while here, *alive*.

I think that basically, and from the very beginning (as a young man, before the monastery), Tom was a 'Body Poet'. I think that the spirit of Eros had finally reclaimed him in his last years — that he was open to touch others in the concrete, the immediate, the (if you will) existential flesh. I think that, at long last, he had 'let go' for the free fall that comes with the final acceptance, the trust, and love of one's own person. . . . He was 'at home with/in creation'.

And, to many, this two-sided face of Thomas Merton appeared to be the major conflict in his life. As a monk and artist, he had a need for solitude. But after prolonged periods of the true joy of such spirituality and creativity, there seemed always to follow an utter loneliness and need for human contact. And the conflict of these dual needs was intensified because Tom was a very warm and friendly human being, and, although admittedly shy, an outgoing sociable person who enjoyed the company of others. It is true that he desired to realize his highest calling, the spiritual life of a contemplative monk — his primary reason for being — but he could not deny the real nature of his personality either. He was someone who appreciated the good things in life—*people*, and all the beautiful doings they were about.

This is no doubt the reason I was privileged to spend so much time with him those last few years, like the picnics we had there out in the monastery woods at Monks Pond. They were get-togethers with no more notice than a postcard carrying a scribbled message from the hermitage, or a P.S. to a letter announcing some visitor (poet, publisher, philosopher, friend) was on the way and "come visit with us by the lake." And other such ways. —But of this, more later.

The above too much for what I was after here . . . but comes back to my thinking of Tom as a 'Body Poet'. —In a few words, to give back a piece of what I got from him those long years, his "cure" for me. As best I can word it, what Tom called *A Mini-Sermon To Those With Poor Appetites*:

"Do not suppress the moan in your throat.

"Life . . . eat or be eaten by it.

"In eating, allow the little groans and humphs of taste-bud appreciation.

"Don't stifle health in the cause of manners.

"Slurp . . . slurp . . . back-of-the-hand wet mouth wipes, the joy of eating.

"A *meal* can cause the whole dance of torso-rocking, knee-jig-gling, foot-tapping, head-bobbing, mouth-full-of-food burst of laughter . . . the pure complete "Yes" to gift . . . the chomp chomp *umm good* lip-puckered "Aaahhhh!" to life.

"And the *friction of it* (living open) will wear you away to nothing . . . so gone you are . . . eaten up . . . food to universe mouth.

"A *dying* that's pure . . . and a giving, not being *taken away*.

"Yah! Yah! —the joy of it.

"Passing thru . . . a bite for Buddha . . . swallowed in Yahweh . . . consumed in the Flaming Christ."

End of home homily. But that was it: Thomas Merton giving up his Body 'to be eaten by creation.' —And what a tasty offering. Pure Gift. True Eucharist (in thanksgiving, gratitude for Being)! . . . what his Living was.

And after that brief burst of excited humorous sermoning, Tom went on to tell me that all artists and their works (you, as well as myself included here) represent the anguish and frustration — really the suffering and the joy — of a human trying to express, to realize transcendence (maybe contemplation a better word) in art. And the beauty of this is "the grand noble attempt and fully human failure to become divine in doing so!"

This is always the wish, the need, the *love* of the artist: to communicate, to reveal the inexpressible, the ineffable, in the concrete . . . "to give Body images, symbols, as 'evidence' of Spirit."

Art is no more than the 'residue-evidence' of that journey to another country, contemplation — what is left behind as 'rag-remnants' of the trip. And the artwork, the finished 'good beauty piece' may be looked upon as a human achievement only if viewed simultaneously as a 'failure-divine'!

Art is the doorslam goodbye to that other unseen side of the wall — that thin 'stepping-over' line between body-spirit, immanence-transcendence, existence-being. And all that we are left with, all that we see is "this side of the door now closed to the exit"—the individual going to person, something to nothing. "And where, who is the artist now?"

I must have had a perplexed look on my face when Tom finished this little 'novice lecture' on art and the artist. He noticed my confusion and in that impatient hurried way he had when experiencing someone's incomprehension of something so very obvious to him, Tom continued, but now talking in quick spurts and gesturing with his hands, all the time moving in sort of a pace-dance away then back to me: "You see, for some mysterious reason, throughout all of history, eh . . . humankind has thought it necessary, and *proper*, to leave its mark on the world. That kind of stuff. — as if that were some sort of *jus-ti-fi-ca-tion* for our having been here . . . to leave a 'deposit of good' behind as our gift (due payment) to God. —Some concrete contribution, worthy treasure, a working tool for our salvation(?) . . . Great ideas, books, artworks, landmarks, spiritual *examples* (you know: messages, ways, theologies, lessons, ideals, all those heroic and saintly models). . . . That's the accepted understanding of having lived a good life! —And by God, there's proof, eh? . . . and best of all: the proof is concrete, is demonstrable. It can be used to work for us!"

And here Tom stopped, only a few feet away, his voice becoming more determined, a little stronger. Looking me straight in the eye, he said, "Well . . . to Hell with all that!

"If anyone thinks it appropriate that I leave an epitaph as a mark or monument of evidence of my having been here (for some reason or purpose), and as testimony of some contribution made to the world . . . then let it be this:

"Go out! — without leaving a trace. No physical clue that I've been here. The body completely converted to spirit!

"But O . . . I'm *here* alright.

"I'm spirit — and you'll never get rid of me.

"But damned if you'll ever be able to *use* me.

"Because I'm forever raining on you, washing you with my eternal presence, my holy spirit . . . (what each one of us has to be able to say).

"And Ha! —the divine wit of it.

"You don't know *who* it is, or *if* it is . . . when, where, or how I touch you.

"Unawares, consciously, your questions:

"Who was it curled back my lips in a smile?

"Wherefore come that joy passing through me?

"Who (what) was it teared me with beauty just then?

"Why now this joyous gulp of love?

"My *legacy* — that's what I leave you . . . by not leaving you, ever.

"My mark on this world is that *there is no mark*.

"My contribution to you is my grand refusal to die!

"You've got me on your hands forever . . . on your hands . . . in your heart . . . the tip of your tongue . . . the words from your mouth . . . the light of your eye . . . the *glint in your think* . . . . —Whatever gooses you to life! and kills the death blahs!

"It is the resurrection of a body who never died.

"Life eternal. Pure spirit."

His voice ended in a hush of exhalation. And for an instant Tom's eyes were locked to mine. Until he noticed that tears had filled my bottom lids, ready to roll down my cheeks — and he turned away quickly.

I ran the heels of my hands across my eyes, drying them, and made a slight sound, clearing my throat.

Tom, a little embarrassed I think by the whole situation, turned back around with that big smile of his. "Hey, what the heck. All this arty talk and stuff," waving his hands, then gesturing out the open door of the hermitage, "with all that beauty waiting for us in the woods and all. Take a walk, eh?"

—And what I'd better get up from this typewriter and do now. Because Tom's words that day, his personal expression of *revelation* . . . I hold with me this morning, and will take to the grave. There is no repeat here of the 'content of his say' (what I so feebly tried to restate above); it was more than that. In an experience of true communication — really *communion* — it is more than the 'what', more than the 'how' . . . it is the *who* of the spoken word. The ineffable *Presence*!

Yes.

———————◆———————

Presence!

That last word keeps 'announcing' itself. It is what has kept me here now for almost twelve hours. Long since the monks down at the monastery have completed their choral prayers of *Vigils* (3:15), *Lauds* (5:45), *Terce* (7:30) this morning. Fast approaching noon and *Sext* at 12:15. . . time enough to close this 'spontaneous Say' to Tom's death.

Strange, but I keep expecting poetry to happen here. But again, maybe — this is not the time or place for poetry but "exactly what is," as Jack Kerouac used to say to us . . . what I have been putting off so long: the concrete fact and details of Tom's death and what followed. Too painful.

The Deathday — 10th of December 1968 — and Dan Walsh informing me of the 'how of it' with Tom that same afternoon (reported a few words back). And what followed in the wake.

Neither of us knew the exact circumstances of the death for several hours. All that we were sure of is that Tom was in Thailand to address an international gathering of theologians — until I happened upon:

Found Death Notice

For good reason, the monk was there.
A meeting of Asian Catholic Abbots in Bangkok.
That morning a 'prepared paper' delivered and all monks (with
    questions) eagerly awaited evening session.
After lunch, retired to his room for the meridian.
Then, a shout heard in his cottage —
(All thinking they imagined the cry).
Later found lying on floor, on back, in pajamas.
An electric fan lying across his chest, the switch still on.
A deep burn, some cuts, on right side of arm.
Also, back of head bleeding slightly.
A nun (with medical experience) quickly at his side.
Already dead. Quite evident.
A Thai doctor, then another, arrive.
Exact cause of death difficult to determine.
Victim could have showered, then a heart attack (near fan).
Falling, knocked fan against self.
Or, barefoot on stone floor, (maybe) a fatal electric shock.
Complete investigation by police.
Permission readily given monks to dress body.
First towelled, then robe and scapular, before body laid out on bed.

Then six hour (6 PM till 1:30 AM) constant vigil by monks, rosary and
    psalter recited.
American Army arrives.
Take body to their hospital.
In Bangkok.

Thomas Merton.
Dead.
December 10, 1968

I have just stopped writing for a moment to look at the postcard thumb-tacked to the wall beside me. The one from Tom that
arrived in the mail just two days after his death, dated December 3,
1968 and posted from Ceylon. The picture side is a photo of a
native riding in a bullock cart past a large, white-domed temple.
The blank side is addressed to me at the college and is filled with
his small European script:

> *Dear Ron & Sally*
>
> *There is no place on earth to compare with Ceylon.*
> *The central mountains are a real paradise. I have*
> *seen a lot of it & met many v. nice people — would*
> *love to live here!! But tomorrow I have to move on.*
> *Best wishes & blessings for Christmas.*
>
> *Tom*

would love to live here!! —These words written to me a week before,
and received, two days after his death. With two exclamation
points! . . . the utter 'irony' and 'sadness' of it all.

I have been reading his last words to me over and over for five
days now. And in complete selfishness, I am sometimes angry . . .
feeling that I have been cheated somehow . . . that this person who
means so much to my life has been taken away forever . . .
—I know: shameful. But that's how it is, still.

Also, right below it on the wall, the Western Union telegram
from Brother Patrick (Tom's secretary down at Gethsemani) delivered two days later, dated 14 Dec 1968.

Not exactly how things turned out.

TISSA - DAGOBA
AND TYPICAL
BULLOCK CART

Ceylon
Dec 3.

ARD
MAIL

Dear Ron & Sally
There is no place on earth to
compare with Ceylon. The
central mountains are a
real paradise. I have seen
a lot of it too & met nearly
v. nice people – would love to
live here!! But tomorrow I
have to move on. Best wishes
& blessings for Christmas.
Tom.

Prof Ron Seitz.
Bellarmine College
2000 Norris Pl.
Louisville, Ky
40205
USA

Published by Charles Subasinghe, Hotel Taprobane Book Shop, Colombo.

MR AND MRS RON SEITZ, RECIPIENTS
2161 WINSTON LVILLE

FUNERAL MASS FOR FATHER MERTON 10:00 TUESDAY
17TH THIS TELEGRAM WILL ADMIT RECIPIENT. RSVP

Abbot Flavian and several monks went to Louisville to receive Tom's body. They then took it to New Haven (near the Abbey of Gethsemani) where

> the coffin opened
> to his brothers bending close—
>   silent now   those lips

the body was identified.

The casket was closed again, this time for good, then taken to the Abbey of Gethsemani. Rather than a morning funeral Mass as scheduled in Brother Pat's telegram, the liturgy and burial services were pushed back till late afternoon.

Our Lady of Gethsemani Trappist-Cistercian Abbey, Trappist, Kentucky.

And the events of that afternoon and early evening are already blurring in my memory — at this time, maybe mercifully so.

I recall the far anxious drive out to the monastery from Louisville taking longer than usual, almost two hours. And then the mulling around of many people in the hall of the guesthouse: some faces familiar as friends of Tom for all the twenty-six years he was a monk, a few others from his days at Columbia and earlier days in New York, and those, like myself, who had come to know him later, the last ten or fifteen years of his life, and still others more recently introduced to the man and his work. The gathering arrived from all parts of the country, many on short notice and under difficult conditions.

I recognized a few monks who had moved elsewhere, and a few who had left the order to begin other vocations. It was an uneasy nervous time; a smile did not come easy with my handshake hello.

Moving into the renovated church for the funeral Mass, I knelt quickly and moved my eyes from the small shiny pebbles in the new concrete floor to the large dark wooden beams high up at the ceiling — anything to avoid looking at the casket sitting in the center of the church at the foot of the altar. The sounds and movements of the liturgy went on muffled and hazy to my ears and eyes. I did not participate.

Slow words and images moved my head and heart

> his head sunk heavy
> lying still on the satin—
> hear the monks chanting

Haiku. The short spontaneous poems that Tom and I so loved. "Little prayers," he sometimes called them. —This time, though, more solemn than our quick Zen quips in the woods, out at the hermitage:

"Good! Like tiny pieces of candy on the tongue," he said one morning as I was dropping them like pebbles into Monks Pond. Smiles plopping into ripples of laughter on the water. —No gloom then.

My shroud frown darkening the pew now. What Tom especially wouldn't want in death — some kind of incense-wailing over his

*Monastery church at the Abbey of Gethsemani. View from
visitor guest balcony.*

coffin, all that weepy mourning, sad tears and sinking gloom, the
black of it. And why I'm sure (and glad) that his brother monks
gave him a *white* celebration. Because Tom's death was his birth, his
end his beginning, his goodbye a final yea-say hello of joy and vic-
tory — pure poetry — holy and clean and true . . . and (finally) as
he always wanted: *One with love and beauty and creation in God.*

So, down there in the Abbey church for Tom's funeral Mass,
there would not be any of us "interrupting the smiles with our
sobs" because his brothers, the good monks, were *Hallelujahing*!
The Abbot welcoming us with open arms, smiling, "Lord no. Won't
be any of that sadface weeping. We're not that way about it down
here. —Father Louis' death . . . . Why, we'll be coming out white
and joyful!"

Those words echoed now in the soft voice of Father Abbot
wavering on the air as he spoke the homily. Pieces of it, a sentence
here and there, entering my ear . . . "a younger Brother, even a boy-

ish Brother, who could have lived a hundred years without growing old . . . we laughed at him, and with him, as we would a younger Brother, still we respected him as the spiritual father of our souls."

And then, as if Father Flavian's eyes were piercing my chest to read the Epitaph already etched there: "His passing is a great loss. However, we know that it is not a complete loss. He has left his mark deep . . . and it will be with us for years to come, for he planted it in the hearts of a generation, and God willing, it will be planted for generations to come."

Those words prophetic — no need to remember them. And the *why* of me, this very moment, talking you this book: the task I was 'called' to, and which, unknowingly I had begun still kneeling there after the Mass was over and everyone else was filing out of the church.

Then the burial service out in the gathering dark, alongside the high stone church. *Vespers*. The bells — one by one the gray tolls falling upon the heads of the monks surrounding the casket as the light rain began sleeting as it fell slanting the cold air to *ping* the metal lid covering Tom's body.

And I was moving my lips to the words that had entered my eyes as I watched the pallbearers earlier

> so heavy the weight
> held unwelcome in their arms—
> now the grave marker

A last haiku as snow flurries began silently touching the heads all bowed in prayer around the grave.

The sound of one cold crow *caw*, dead to color across the sky. As the scene fades to black in my memory.

Empty.

A lost fly buzz in Tom's hermitage tells me the Tao of this book — distracts my attention so not too quick to set the mind on what's to come, what's to be when all's finally put down as THE SAY!

If to leave this desk to walk Gethsemani's fields and woods for just the joy of it seems the Way just now — then why not answer?

What is this loneliness that has followed me into solitude — this time and place provided to put words on paper, to do 'the work'?

Am I speaking this because even now in this still night hour (again, to begin) — I see Tom's face filling the empty hour caught framed by time . . . my space of flesh hung heavy with waiting for his presence to go 'out' to nothing, all eternity ONE?

Mark the void with sound to smear the silence and portrait his person . . . my calling?

This motioned body printing the page with language, blacking white with noise — to initial Being with his existence?

The what, the why, the Who — here announced:

This voice picks up the toll to tell the tale, what needs be said.

Amen

Part Two

. . . is my end

45

DECEMBER 8, 1988

AND SO BACK HERE AGAIN, in my writing cell in the basement, surrounded by all the reminders of the past twenty years.

December. Cold, as always. —But this time the room warmed some (a small electric heater on the desk near my hands as I write) . . . not as it was that long night and morning a week after Tom's death, when I sat here hunched to the zero weather breathing through the concrete wall, the outside air swirling with snow.

A long time to live and work in the same place, the same space — this home, this study. Almost as long as Tom's stay at his home — the monastery, the Abbey of Gethsemani.

But both houses have changed in those long slow, short quick years. Here, of course, more quiet (our three sons not boys but men grown and gone), yet more crowded — at least this room, filling with books books books . . . most by Tom, about Tom, ones we read together, others exchanged or recommended, with scribbled marginal notes "IMP!!!" in all of them.

A lone framed photograph hangs on the wall directly in front of me. A picture of two serene, almost smiling (Buddha-like) faces — Tom and the Dalai Lama standing side-by-side — still, their eyes

Fr. Louis Merton and the Dalai Lama, November 4, 1968. One of the last photos before Thomas Merton's death on December 10, 1968.

clear and open, kindly looking at me . . . as if to say, "Okay, Ron, we're watching now; time to get on with what must be done."

A tall metal filing cabinet stands in the far corner of the room. There, four full drawers contain most of my TOM STUFF, printed in large black letters on a piece of white cardboard scotch-taped to the top of the cabinet — the *Merton Materials*.

All of those exchanged writings, letters, notes, photographs, drawings — the entire collection of which Tom agreed would be entrusted to me, to do with whatever I chose. Whether this were to be a book-of-sorts published ten or twenty years after Tom's death, or just turned over to some library of Mertonia a short period after mine.

So, sitting here now late at night, I can only stare at the locked drawers of that cabinet, debating whether to open the vault of that 'too personal' material and gather it into a book-portrait of our ten-year friendship, or just leave them closed. Am I brave or fool enough to rely upon the power and gift of my imagination to make come alive the part of Tom Merton's life that I shared. At the moment, the first appears too formidable. As to the second: this room, this time, this solitude tells me to 'trust my muse' (at least for the next few days) and to put down here, as quickly as possible, my memory vision — our *Song for Nobody*.

———◆———

To write of Tom is not easy. Not the same as an author going about a run-on celebratory chant in praise of his hero. —That, a self-conscious literary bone-in-the-throat for anyone with a taste for clear cold water to rinse the eyes of precious rhetoric.

One approaches Merton with a bare branch clean of bark, and dare not touch, or even point. —The man not that *apart* from you.

"Good Lou-ie" (Father Louis) — what his brother monks called him — stands full-bodied and open before you, with no apparent *hidden otherness* to decipher. But that initial 'take' is somewhat myopic and illusory. The full laughter of his presence is empty of pretense. The white of his wide-eyed look peels you of any protective shield of 'distancing' that most arm themselves with in preparation for a one-on-one meeting of wills.

Tom's receptive vulnerable acceptance (without conscious intent) of a person as is . . . strips the other of any combative guise adopted to avert the converting influence anticipated by this face-to-face 'touch' with a man of such spiritual stature.

So the first thing for me to come to tonight is that . . . I am *home!* —There is no more 'holy place to be' than here in this small basement room, sitting in this straight-backed wooden chair, asking you to listen, to suffer another one of those people who purport to have *the word*.

No danger there for you: I come in ignorance. Dues paid in full . . . by years of vanity.

If I speak anything of truth, beauty, goodness here — it is no work of mine. My contribution (if we be 'blessed' enough to experience that) will depend upon my being open enough, empty enough to be *used* . . . as a voicebox of truth, an instrument of beauty, a vessel of goodness. And with your kindness, with my courage, it may happen. Community of language, of ideas can take place. But far more importantly, we might just be graced with the communion of experience . . . if I be humble enough, and you be patient enough, and together we be in love.

Maybe I should title these words (if that even necessary): "Who Tom Speaks Me!" . . . Doing this, to be sure, with the trust and affection that what I say will be in 'the Spirit of Thomas Merton'.

There is a very good chance (possibly a certainty at that) — considering who I am and my qualifications to "inform you as to what Tom Merton was about in his life and work" — a chance that I'll miss the mark a long way.

But to give it some kind of a shot at all . . . I'll go at this thing as a Zen archer! —That is: I'll not aim!

Just trust the bow (my body) and the arrow (Tom's spirit) . . . and hope to *touch*!

—If you don't mind being target to such spiritual sport.

———————◆———————

The pen drops from my cramped hand and I switch to the typewriter to continue this run-on elegiac mourn for Merton.

The speed of this instrument coupled with the improvisational image rhythms of my head and heart at this moment produce a kind of spontaneous verbal play at poetry . . . "whicheverway the blues move me," as Tom used to say.

No apology. Just a warning.

So now I sit eyes closed with fingers dancing these keys unawares what comes next as the letters click click to words words type-tapping across the page line by line to a soft bell ting that lifts my hand to push the carriage back to continue the paper roll that runs the rhythm of this language laugh long letter to Tom tonight till morning as together we go the same say, Amen.

It's now near midnight and this unchartered narrative winds its way unchecked — no chronology, structure, sequence, or form, other than the nuances of my mood and mind at whatever instant of this solo sing.

As it is with all home movies: the projectionist stops the reel of flickering motion at will, and offers, however unwelcome, obtrusive commentary — a belated 'voice-over' due to the near impossibility of juxtaposing abstract and concrete simultaneously without silencing one side of this single-voiced chorus.

So let this be one long unravelling vision *living* — the breath of palpable presence born as we go. No photo nostalgia of recall, but a Zen sketch signature singing.

>   . . . Tom.
>   His death far down the tunnel of time — December 1968.
>   And what I say now, twenty years after, growing old, near death too in my grizzle beard (this haze of hair glooms me teary in my longdays failure not poeting my life).
>   Me with my endless scribble of pain that no one cares or wants to read because this not the time or place for *written word*. No sacred space for the solitude of silence . . . . I sit and crow on the junkheap dungpile of crumbled culture that never was. Squat and scrawl other long cables to what Ace?
>   Here, in this lone cell, speaking to no one but the long coil of my own ear. And to Tom, my audience of one, who might understand the hidden rhythms of this cryptic message, who hovers, breathes, and envelopes the void which bears me along a speck of consciousness in the whole wash of it.
>   Tom — who slipped the skin (trapped existence) of his encapsulated "I" . . . the illusory identity of *individual*, and gone back to the cosmic soup of All/ One . . . Being.
>   Home.

Conscious, imagine: here project moving portrait of Merton. Not the Tom of biography — dead print on dead page . . . historical corpse. But the voice *live* as speaking.

Enough the reader following (with a yawn) my synapse syntax. Details are the life of it. Back to the action.

Just darken the room by closing the eyes and listen to the sweet high single-syllabled music for a memory vision . . . *Song for Nobody.*

———◆———

>   On the last day of October 1958, under the sign of the Scorpion, in the year of cold peace, and out in the shade of a giant ginkgo tree in the center of Kentucky, I came into the world . . . of Thomas Merton.
>   And if you came this way, taking a route from Prades to Bermuda to St. Antonin to Oakham to London to Cambridge to Rome to New York to Columbia to Corpus Christi to St. Bonaventure to the Cistercian Abbey of the poor men who labor in Gethsemani — a Trappist monastery set deep in the hills of Nelson County, Kentucky — on that cold winter day of December 10, 1941, and stood at the

end of the long tree-lined entrance road, in the shadow of the stone arch of the gatehouse, beneath the two large latin words *Pax Intrantibus* (Peace To All Who Enter), and rang the bell, waiting to leave one world and enter another . . . you would have been a young man of twenty-six, a person by the name of Thomas Merton.

But if you came this way, taking a different route, from Kentucky on the road South to Florida beach to Southwest and Huachuca to Old Mexico to the Far West coast L.A. to Frisco to cross continent to Boston to New York to Kentucky full circle seventeen years later on a sunny morning the last day of October 1958, and stood in the same place, waiting to step through the same door . . . you would have been a younger man of twenty-three, someone named Ron Seitz.

No, it is not always the same. The one "would have to put off sense and motion" . . . the other was not quite ready for that.

Thomas Merton was here "to kneel where prayer has been valid" . . . Ron Seitz was here more "to verify, instruct himself, inform curiosity or carry report."

—Enough. Not it. Not what I want.

Got to get up and out of here, away from this deadening climate of accumulated history and head for the monastery to wipe clean my vision, to begin again fresh with my memory — the only instrument of inspiration and creativity to compose a portrait of the Thomas Merton I knew.

This, what I had expected when I called the Abbey `this afternoon and made arrangements to pack it up and head out there in the morning if the writing did not go well here.

The plan: spend an entire day at the monastery, beginning with the three o'clock wake-up and following the monks' daily schedule of prayers and liturgy. Their work time, my work time . . . but mine spent exploring the Abbey grounds, wandering wherever the spirit leads me, composing a 'memory journey' in my head as I go, recalling and recording some of the many experiences that Tom and I shared in our ten good years together.

As I raise my fingers from these keys

———◆———

December 9, 1988

It is a cold December morning, almost nine o'clock, the winter air crisp and clear. I am happy to be away from the city and here at the Abbey of Gethsemani. There is something clean and quiet settling over me as I sit on a small wooden 'meditation bench' beneath the giant ginkgo tree in the monastery front garden. Above me the branches are thick, black, and bare. Not at all as it was that sunny morning, the last day of October some thirty years ago, when I sat here waiting to meet Thomas Merton for the first time.

I remember the countryside afire with the woods flashing yellow, red, and orange in gusts of warm wind as the oriental fan-shaped leaves of the ginkgo had blossomed to their full light and fell fluttering golden in some kind of petal shower brushing my head and shoulders before settling softly in my lap and, almost by direction, one bright leaf landing in the palm of my right hand cupped open atop my knee. —The right place at the right time: my blessing.

Around nine-thirty Tom was to pick up his mail at the Abbey Post Office in the right wing of the gatehouse building, the door just a few feet from where I now sit. We would meet there.

Very old gingko tree in courtyard of Gethsemani Abbey.

Turning to face the square gray-stone old guest house across the garden, I ask myself once more why Tom included me when he invited five young artists from Louisville to visit him. Being the only poet to accompany four painters had been intimidating: more would be expected of me in the give-and-take of conversation.

And that had been the case when Tom did join us under the ginkgo tree. One of the young artists who had read and revered Merton had, upon first seeing the famous monk, remarked: "Hey, he's shorter than I thought he'd be — not as thin as I'd pictured him."

A remark that Tom overheard as he approached us. Causing him to mock-mimic his physical stature not matching holy card images of sanctity: "Got to don Gandhian garb of lean loin cloth and sunkcheek hunger hunch as I sandal me way to bare ricebowl breakfast" — winking at me for company in verbal play as he laughed at his own cryptic humor.

But I was as dumb as the others in response, and could only grin at this display of poetic slapstick.

—This incident from our first meeting, I remember best . . . sitting beneath the ginkgo tree.

Up from the bench, through the gatehouse, and out the entrance door, I see the tombstones of the monastery's Secular Cemetery to the right of me. This small plot of graves and stone markers is reserved for 'friends and neighbors' of the Trappist community: a mix of age and size, a lopsided graveyard square pointing its granite fingers crooked to heaven.

> in death's deep burial ground
> the stones slant heavy, sinking
> (weed imprisoned)
>
>> weathered faces gazing
>> haphazard
>> at the world
>
> and over every rise comes
> the unwelcome breath
> of marble

Unique place. The sister of Jefferson Davis, the President of the Confederacy, is buried here. So is one of Abraham Lincoln's teachers; and the final resting place of this man is strangely connected to that of another teacher — Dan Walsh. Good Father Doctor Dan . . . Tom's mentor at Columbia University, professor of philosophy and ordained instrument of conversions.

Walking a few steps inside and along the entrance wall I stop and stand above the small gray marble marker, plain, with a decorative flower in the right lower corner, and read the inscription:

> ### REV. FATHER DANIEL C. WALSH
> ### NOV. 3, 1903
> ### AUG. 28, 1975

and hear the word, "Dan" — the sound of my whispered voice bringing in a rush all the memories of this man . . . what he had to do with the ultimate destiny of Thomas Merton. And myself. And how many thousands of others, God knows.

I turn away quickly, blanking the vision, and begin walking among the other markers in the cemetery. Here too are several of the plain iron crosses that line the hill of the Trappist Cemetery. A stone angel standing atop a wide concrete base stops me. The figure is of a young girl with short wings protruding from her back. With downcast eyes, she has her hands folded high beneath her chin. I am not looking at the angel as such, but of the etched stains of weathered age on the stone face. I reach up and place the palm of my right hand against the cheek. It is hard; the cold spreads through my fingers. —And, again, I am aware of time . . . how ephemeral and fleeting life is. Reminding me of what Tom had once said about poetry when I had criticized his recent work as being too topical, the images not being concrete and universal and timeless as his early poems were. And he had shocked me with the suddenness of his revelation that "nothing is permanent . . . not even time."

The thought moves my eyes to another marker nearby — a tall concrete cross with iron rods rusting through the crumbling arms, its base rising out of a heavy immovable stone slab, in silence saying:

HERE BEFORE YOU ARE,
HERE AFTER YOU WERE.

The same. "What the thick stones of these old monastery walls have been breathing us all these years," Tom's words echoing inside me.

Out of the cemetery and walking down the entrance road from the gatehouse now, I cross over into the grass until I come to three metal lawn chairs beneath a tree near the enclosure wall. The sky is still gray and the tree and the stones look the same, but it is different. I feel a weight lift from my chest. This is a special place. A spot of light lingers here.

This is where I first met Bob Lax, Tom's longtime best friend from his Columbia days. —Bob Lax, the unassuming humble and most humorous companion of Tom those many long years in the monastery where he was so alone and denied the intimacy of understanding and appreciation of a fellow artist . . . what Bob seemed to give him in his letters and infrequent visits.

A very good poet now, Bob was passing through from the West after working with the Indians for a short while, on his way back to his self-imposed exile somewhere in Greece — his retreat from "the zoo of secular hurry" as Tom put it. I had received a note from Tom saying that he wanted me to meet and know this good man, so why not a get-together down at the monastery.

Okay.

———◆———

So, loaded the backseat of the car with food that Sally had prepared, stopped along the way to buy a couple bottles of wine, and made the long winding drive on old Bardstown Road from Louisville down to the Abbey.

Turning onto the entrance road I saw Tom standing beside the wall beneath a tree, the strap of his camera looped around his neck, talking to what appeared to be one of the local farmers — a thin gawky man, looking taller than he is, in bib overalls, balding and big-nosed, open-mouthed grinning and full of teeth (horse-faced almost in his rural stance). And as I parked the car, got out, and

From the desk of
Father Louis, ocso

Friday.

Dear Ron.

Dick Sisto said you might come
out with him Monday. Do that:
Bob Lax will be here by then. Hope
we can have a picnic. Will be
expecting you all about 11.30 unless
I hear otherwise.

Best

Tom

*Bob Lax, lifelong friend of
Tom Merton since their days at
Columbia University in 1935.*

approached them, ready to ask when Bob Lax would get there — Tom proudly introduced this "anonymous poet-artist, monk-in-hiding" to me.

Bob's spontaneous laugh and open-palm welcome instantly justified Tom's description of him: "a man free enough to see the beauty of, and run off with, a circus." (While a writer for a New York magazine, Lax's assignment was to cover the circus visiting town. He did not report back to the office that day, or the next, but traveled with the troupe for several months — then wrote a book of poems about it.)

I immediately understood their lifelong friendship that expressed itself in an exchange of cryptic 'anti-letters' when apart, and created a mutual wonder-field of eye contact, glints of recognition accompanied by continual bursts of laughter and headnods of glad agreement about most everything, which I began witnessing before the handshakes hello were completed.

But our introduction was somewhat awkward and embarrassing because both Bob and I immediately complimented each other on our poetry (examples of which were soon to appear in Tom's new literary magazine, *Monks Pond*). Tom had shown Bob a long poem, "Vaudeville Dancer" (written to my dad), while they were waiting for me to arrive (and which Bob still held curled in his hand, now and then looking down at it with a nod, grinning). And for several months Tom had been showing me some of Bob's most recent work in 'concrete poetry' (an experimental minimalist form then)—which on first seeing I had made the naive remark that, "It looks easy to me, that kind of thing." Which provoked the reply, "Think so, eh? Give it a try, then come tell me." One of the few times (but not the first or last) that I had seen Tom hurt and possibly angered, impatient with my ignorance — his face tightening as the words came out quick and curt . . . but only for an instant. Then once more the warm open expression. —And Bob again with toothy grin as Tom took quick snapshots of both of us.

Then, as we sat there in those three metal lawn chairs talking and laughing (we had a half-hour before we were to drive down to Monks Pond and meet the others — Naomi Burton, Dick Sisto, John Loftus — for the picnic), I thanked Bob for being instrumental in bringing Tom to Gethsemani.

"Oh, it wasn't much," he said. "Just a bit of advice from someone a wit wiser as we took a walk along Sixth Avenue one night a long time ago. New York's a good place for that sort of thing, 1940 a good time" . . . referring to their conversation over twenty-five years before when Bob had asked Tom, "What do you want to be, anyway?"

And Tom had answered with the usual "writer or teacher or artist" . . . but then admitted, "I guess I want to be a good Christian."

But Bob came right back with, "What do you mean by that? . . . Why don't you come straight out and say it: *You want to be a saint!*"

The statement unnerving Tom, "How can you expect me to do that? I can't . . ."

His rejection interrupted by Bob, "By wanting to — that's all that's necessary. Don't you believe that God'll let you be who you were created to be? . . . All you have to do is desire it."

Follow your ecstasy, I said to myself as Tom was smiling now at the memory of that longago incident and Bob's brief casual account of it.

Their conversation then wended its way in and out of various subjects, breaking off here and there to make handheld leaps to familiar territory without a pause or direct connection. I just let my ear follow along from this to that, picking up on bits that fit. Until an abrupt break in their rapid-fire give-and-take, when Bob reached down and pulled up a long strand of grass, holding it a few inches from his mouth, and looked at Tom without smiling. "You know, it just dawned on me the other day," he said slowly, "—our generation is over."

There was a moment of silence, with both of them looking into each other's eyes . . . and Tom, with just a slight nod, pursed his lips in agreement.

> sunken cheek and blue-jawed they
> galloped through dives damning
> Buddha a pregnant
> book Zen
>
> my Apocalypse howling
> generation now
> old and
> spent

My poem . . . that I had just given Tom a few months ago, and
that he was going to publish in *Monks Pond.* —But that's not what I
meant at all . . . what Bob had just said. His words struck me hard:
the thought of their group, its *voice*, being over. Because, although
twenty years younger, I considered myself to be one with them . . .
their vision was still *new.* —What I was referring to in my poem was
that youthful rebellious spirit of our poetry the past fifteen years.
Ginsberg and "Kerouac."

I heard the word come out of my mouth, unexpectedly.

"Uh, Tom said I'd be in the same issue with Kerouac," I added,
trying to cover the embarrassment of my outburst.

"Kerouac, ol' Jack . . . yeah, he sent me a couple little poems for
my second issue. Jack's a good friend of Bob here, eh Bob?" laughing.
—"You know what he told me in his letter? . . . Said he was walking
the beaches of Florida trying to get inspiration for a new novel."

"Florida, eh? . . . Now that's *the* place to be — real creative climate I'd say," Bob laughed. " —But Jack's still a sweet sensitive soul
. . . in spite of all that mess these past few years."

"Bob was one of the first to publish Kerouac, when he was editor of *Jubilee* quite a few years back," Tom said, knowing that I
thought a lot of his writing. "They sat up all night one New Year's
Eve reading *Finnegans Wake* aloud to each other . . . . Took him to a
monastery once for a few days too, didn't you, Bob?"

"Tried to," Bob said, his mind apparently on something else.
"Tell you a good story about Kerouac," grinning at both of us. "You
see, Jack has a real tender love for animals. And we were walking
along the street, somewhere in New York I don't know, and there
was this old guy on the corner with a cardboard box, selling little
kittens out of it. Well, that was enough to stop Jack. He looked
down into the box at all the cats, about five of them, climbing on
top of each other, and he asked the man which one was the best.
'Aw, anyone of these,' the old man said, pointing to four of them
jumping all around.

"'What about that little one over there in the corner?' Jack asked.

"'Aw, something's wrong with him. Maybe crippled or something, I dunno.'

"'Good. I'll take him,' Jack said, walking off with the little kitten
all curled in the crook of his arm, happy as he could be. . . . He's a
tender soul, Jack is. —Just a little screwed-up right now," Bob said,
looking away.

"Well, Ron won't argue with you about that. Read everything he's written, and took him seriously about all that 'On the Road' stuff. —Only he outdid him with the hitchhike traveling thing. Wait till you read what he sent me for the Contributor Notes section of *Monks Pond*," Tom laughed.

Tom was referring to his letter a few months back:

Dear Ron:

Thanks so much for the poems. They were very good ones. Maybe I am prejudiced because I read them sitting up listening to fabulous Coltrane records I acquired. But the poems are real good and I hope to use a whole slew of them in maybe second or third issue of Monks Pond.

Now you gotta give me biography stuff for the contributors' notes, and if wish to express some goddam opinions about the universe that is fine because that is what the other poets have been doing.

We got a new broadminded abbot so maybe it is easier for everyone to come on out and sit around the lakes, so come some time in spring and bring beautiful redhaired wife she needs freshair. Babies also need freshair. etc.

Will send first issue if I can remember.

Best

Tom

And's true. I sent stacks of poems. Most of them I didn't even bother putting my name to. Tom did publish quite a few in the last three issues — eleven; in fact, five of them under someone else's name in the third issue (another one of those "dumb things to do" that irritated him in this unique project).

And the "biographical stuff" that Tom requested in the letter did read like a Kerouac dustjacket blurb:

> born 1935 innocent a baby poet till after gradeschool miracle visions & highschool pole-vaulting natural handsome athlete, then Florida beach Army California Boston far west Huachuca ol Mexico to Kentucky college & out again on the road South Southwest to Coast LA to Frisco & grad school to Majorca Hollywood back in Kentucky

teaching Bellarmine now — poems along the way & grocery paper-
boy caddy landscape lifeguard garbageman gravedigger salesman bar-
tender probation-officer Radio TV factory research carpenter tilesetter
sewers construction executive mailman greenskeeper advertising
industry warehouse teacher writer now lover at 32 & still beautiful &
married a lovely girl Sally & so three boys Dylan Sean Casey

Pieces of which Tom remembered and was reciting singsongy now
to Bob laughing as I waved my arms stop! stop! . . . enough.

"Or I'll turn it around completely on you, Tom, and recite
word-for-word your byfar most beautiful poem, 'Night-Flowering
Cactus'."

Which brought Bob out of his chair and to his feet, pointing his
long arm at Tom with "See, see, I told you so — What'd I say? Your
best work, eh?" . . . his eyes bright and white, mouth wide-open
grinning, then slapping both hands against his thighs: "Everything there is to say. It's all there . . . that poem."

Tom shy, a little uncomfortable, lowering his head to stifle short
breaths of laughter: "Alright now, you guys . . . all even. Give a
poor monk a break. . . . Time to go."

And walking along beneath the trees towards the car I remember reciting one of my recent haiku to Bob (at Tom's request)

> waiting for two monks
> to drag a log up the hill
> he removed his hat

And Bob laughed "Yes!" — clapping his palms together, glancing back at Tom, "your hat, eh?

"Another."

> so quiet the raindrops
> slowly *tap ping* down through leaves
> onto his bald head

Bob tapping his finger on top of his head, then pointing to
Tom: "Gotcha again, eh?" . . . stopping. "One more."

> on winter dead grass
> the bird's skinny little legs
> —far off a dog barks

Upon hearing this last one (my favorite), Bob threw up both arms with "That's it! . . . I just heard the same image from a young Indian girl in South Dakota last week. . . . That's in the air now, up for grabs," — so happy with his discovery and looking over to Tom for his knowing nod.

Bob's response here meaning that the image in my poem was a 'true one' because *not mine* but just passing-thru me at the particular time of writing — all poets being "recording angels sent by God" . . . as Bob stated it in one of his poems.

And that frozen frame of a moment — with Tom standing between us, grinning with pride at the touch Bob had made — that is what I carry with me now of good Lax.

———————◆———————

December — not the time to be sitting in an abandoned metal lawn chair musing upon the past. I push myself up and carry the cold pressure against my back as I walk to where the long entrance road begins curving down to the highway.

Off the pavement and in the grass I see the hill in front of me slanting away from the monastery on one side and rising up to the statue of St. Joseph the top of the knoll the other side. Standing still a moment, with my eyes scanning the Gethsemani landscape, the words of Tom's early poems come to my lips and deep inside my chest his voice announces all of those beautiful nature images speaking themselves, "Here! . . . Here!" — evocative hymns singing *theophany*: "Am Holy, the Sacred . . . that are Thou!"

The crisp clear inner echoes imaged silent now as I walk approaching the large stone crucifix facing the highway the bottom of the hill. I stop and step into the brush surrounding the wide concrete base, to take my hands and part the briar branches spread across and hiding the inscription there. To read:

> **I HAVE SUFFERED THIS**
> **FOR YOU**
> **WHAT HAVE YOU DONE**
> **FOR ME?**

A still cold stare to the gray, almost silver, stone figure of Christ nailed to the cross — my only answer.

I cross the road and head for the dark woods in the distance. Somewhere over the next hill I will find the *Garden of Gethsemani* bronze sculpture among the tall bare trees. And walking, I begin talking to myself (to Merton, really), asking the same question that has been repeating itself since I first arrived early this morning, "Tom, why did you bring me back here?"

Until I am standing in the shadowed woods between the two metal sculpture pieces. Directly facing me is the upright figure of Jesus with head thrown back facing heaven, his arms raised high to clasp both hands across his eyes — an expression of abandoned anguish. A shaft of sunlight slants through the branches above and shines the folds of his gown hanging tight to his chest, a black sheen of bronze announcing his indisputable presence.

Off to the side, behind and to the left of Jesus, is a cluster of three figures reclining on the ground: the Sleeping Apostles. I lean close to see the clean chiseled features of one face. Handsome, so serene . . . cold, unmoving . . . dead? —I could have been the model.

"Agony in the garden," I half whisper. "Whose agony? We apostles," I answer myself, turning away.

Sleeping Apostles in Garden of Gethsemani, *bronze sculpture on the Abbey grounds.*

A long clear stretch of land opens before me as I walk the winding dirt road that leads to Dom Frederick's Lake, now called Monks Pond (named by Merton, later the title of his literary magazine). It is not all that large a pond, but large enough for a decent swim from time to time, (which Tom was known to take advantage of — when he was not busily occupied keeping its banks clear of brush and the likes). A concrete wall bounds one side of it, and this is the site of most of our picnics.

As the road narrows and enters the woods again, I pass an abandoned stone hermitage to the left. Once called St. Enoch's, the one-room hut is now used to store firewood. Years ago I stopped here and lit a small candle set atop the fireplace — a pious attempt to make a shrine of the place, but moreso to produce an effect for an 'artistic' photograph. A failure on both accounts.

Passing another clearing, I walk through some underbrush and reach the water's edge of Monks Pond. Then move along the bank until I come to the concrete wall. I stop, standing in a small spot of shade from a low branch overhang, and rest my arms atop the chesthigh ledge. To look out over the water, stare at the flat shine of

St. Enoch's, abandoned hermitage on Abbey grounds.

the sun on its surface, now frozen with a thin cover of ice, until everything else around me drops away and I am empty and open to the memory of my best moments with Tom Merton — the many get-togethers we had here, at this place (with Sally, Father John, Bob Lax, Tommie O'Callaghan, Naomi Burton, and others).

And what comes now is the memory vision, slowly developing, of our one-on-one picnic, the best and almost last one together, in early May of 1968. I was to begin a brief break from teaching, to do some writing, and I needed his experience to guide me. So, a short note, "Can you help me?"

the 22nd of April dear Tom & thought I would send along a few words. Hope the Easter season has left you joyous and green with all the hills blooming . . . Spring here on campus happened all at once and the classroom must be abandoned to the outdoors young girls and longhairs coloring the walk. . . . I don't know if I told you, or maybe Dan did, about my good fortune for this summer. The College has given me a Sabbatical (sp?) so that I can write. 3½ months of freedom, no teaching and full pay – to see if I have anything to say, to see what I can produce given the chance. I'm on the spot now. . . . Would love to have an hour with you sometime to talk about this before I get started around May 10th. You know, to get some sort of direction and confidence, and maybe a few pointers about how to go with this writing every day, discipline & schedule & patience & hope, etc. – the old pre-game pep talk in the locker room . . . Would still like a picnic & wine & maybe Coltrane if ever you feel up to it . . . Dan got home safe from the riots in Kansas City last week. He gave me a copy of CABLES and I like them much better than when I read them in manuscript. Some sections are as good as anything you've written . . . Well Tom I got to get back for my next class – Kafka today and because of season not too much with it on gloom. Much rather go with Basho or Thomas or cummings – "I thank thee God most for this amazing day, for the leaping greenly spirits of trees, and the true blue dream of sky!" – that kind of stuff . . . so see you.

An immediate Abbey of Gethsemani postcard reply:

Dear Ron:

Thanks for your letter. Yes, I'd love a picnic: about only chance for me however would be Wednesday or Thursday of next week, May Day or May 2. Glad to hear of yr sabbatical! Too bad you have to think you must produce. One does more when there is no obligation to do anything.
See you I hope next week.

> *Best,*
> *Tom*

——————◆——————

As usual, I picked Tom up at the hermitage and we drove down the dirt road, crossed the highway, and then back the other dirt road until we were within walking distance of the lake. We carried the food and drinks down to our usual spot near the wall, cleared a space, and sat down beneath the wide cloudless blue sky. Taking off our caps and shirts, we settled back bare-headed bare-chested, and relaxed.

It was one of those green and growing, fresh-blowing spring days, a week or so before his brief visit out West prior to the longer one planned later that Fall to the Far East. I was about to begin a period of solitude and creativity somewhat similar to his life at the hermitage. What advice could he offer me about such an undertaking?

After opening a couple cans of beer and resting silent a few moments, we propped our arms atop the concrete wall and looked out over the water.

"I can't think of anything more solitary, or lonely, than writing," Tom began, "except prayer, of course." —He paused. "There's nothing to compare to the true joy of the spiritual life, the creative life. While you're totally in it. But, when coming out of it, there's the most desperate gnawing need for human contact."

He stopped, and I didn't think he was going to continue. He seemed to have left me and was thinking about what he had just said.

But this 'condition', the conflict of these dual needs, so very real and human (shared by many of us in different degrees) — is what we had come to talk about that May morning. I knew this . . . and I waited now.

Tom began again by assuring and reassuring me that I must feel absolutely no obligation to write anything the coming months. "If the writing is involved with 'duty' or 'productivity', in a word, *jus-ti-fi-ca-tion* — then you're finished as an artist. If the poems come of their own, if they 'happen' — good! If they don't, there's no way to force it — period."

Then, when he was sure I had gotten the wisdom of that, Tom turned and looked me in the eyes, and selecting each word carefully, (as best I can remember and word it) said:

"Dare let loose the body and speak whatever spirit says first this head of yours.

"Loose the knots and allow your heart to sing whatever asks it.

"No longer hold back or check what enters, touches, and frees to exit as speech-seeds in your talk or writing.

"Because poems are speech-seeds. —Seeds for flowers that can never blossom to statement, explanation, theology, philosophy.

"Because the life-spark spirit that urges you on, pumps these words out, is inexpressible — not to be said, not to be communicated . . . but is here in *communion* only.

"—And touches others, loves them . . . not in what you say, not in what you do, but . . . in *who you are*!

"And who you are is not the self that speaks these words.

"The self you witness here is but an imperfect joyous instrument, whose truth and beauty is its failure to *one with all*!

"—Your off-key out-of-tune impossible attempt to sing Heaven.

"And love the spirit that silences your body."

His voice had stopped and his mouth had closed, but the words still sat there between our eyes.

Struck dumb by what Tom had just done, I was frightened — not fear, but awe.

Then just as quickly as he had begun, he turned back to the lake. And only then did I feel a stirring in my blood, my pulse pumping. Suddenly my mind was a brushfire of thoughts and images. "Enough, Tom, enough!" I wanted to say, but still could not speak.

How long we remained like this, I can't say. Possibly only a moment. —But I knew that something had happened between us and things would never be as they were before. Something wholly new was with us now.

"Like another beer?" Tom asked, smiling.

And that broke it. A rush of relief exhaled from me as I released my held breath. I felt a flow of energy and complete relaxation at the same time. I heard myself laughing. Louder — listening to my voice echo off the water and hang in the woods the other side.

With our shirts back on and sitting down again, Tom went on to tell me that the real challenge, the true commitment, the hard discipline is to have enough courage to "accept who you are." That is, dare be defenseless, vulnerable, open, and porous to life in its entirety.

"Do not protect yourself from life by embracing death!"

Tom explained that I must never cheat myself of an experience by accepting someone else's 'response' as a prejudgment or dilution of the 'firsthand touch' itself. He told me that I must be open always to the possibility, the probability, in fact . . . the inevitability of the goodness, the beauty, the truth, *the holiness of everything in creation!*

"So, you see, no matter what we're saying now in our art — we've got to remember that artists are just 'tuned-in', so to speak, and must remain open and empty to the beauty of creation as it is revealed *through* us. . . . That's why it shouldn't bother you, eh — knowing that the poet never says anything new, original, the first time — that all of this has been known, been said many times before. . . . and *better!*"

Tom looked at me with a little "Heh," laughing, to see if I was riding along with him on this and then turned back to the lake.

"You see," he went on, — "nothing true, good, or beautiful really 'belongs' to any of us. We're just reflectors, refractors, instruments, sounding boards."

Then pausing, as if to remind himself as well as me: "But as writers . . . say-ers (who are *see*-ers), we report again, for the thousandth time, the old 'ever-new' vision of the *now* of it."

Then lowering his voice, his eyes staring straight ahead, "And for sure, our song's been sung. —But maybe not so off-key, so out-of-tune, so wrong-worded, so 'unique' . . . in that no one has failed, as we all must, in such individual ways that are so 'peculiar' to *who we are.*

"So, every few years, a handful of us singers try again the 'old standards'. And if the songs that choose us are the 'true tunes', they will work again — *touch others with spirit!*

"Because the songs are eternal. . . . And we *must* sing them in every age. . . . And we must *listen* to them always.

"Because *all of who we are* . . . is through revelation. — And we would die without these songs . . . which make us *persons* and not 'things'.

"So, Ron, we've got to sing on! We may give out with only one song, but" — Again, Tom stopped abruptly. He had been staring out over the lake as he spoke. Now, turning back to face me, he saw that I had not even opened my can of beer but was just sitting there looking at him, my mouth half open, still unable to speak.

"Hey, come on now," getting to his feet. "We're out here to have a little fun, enjoy ourselves," brushing the seat of his pants. "No more serious sermons in the sun! Drink your beer."

"I . . . was just sitting there . . . looking at him . . . unable to speak." The author at a "singers" picnic with Tom Merton on the Abbey grounds.

And I did that — settling down to eat the lunch Sally packed for us. First, fruit and cheese; then fried chicken, baked beans, and potato salad; finally, German chocolate cake. A big outdoor feast of eating, drinking, relaxing . . . and all the while talking, talking. A conversation, a lesson, an education —Zen Master to young novice experience to end all.

One hour, two hours, then three, and four. On and on — laughing, yelling, whispering, "pome-ing it" while the wind blew, clouds came and went, and the sun, the sun always there beating down on us . . . one in spirit with Van Gogh the south of France: a maelstrom of emotion, creativity, and joy.

This, yes . . . but from time to time our good cheer would be muted by mention of something saddening in the world about us. Martin Luther King had been assassinated just a few days earlier. Tom told me that they had planned to get together at the hermitage the end of the month. And I mentioned again my experiences traveling with King on the Selma March back in 1965 — what a moving and unforgettable privilege to stand with him in front of the Alabama State Capitol in Montgomery that afternoon while thousands of us linked arms and sang together "We Shall Overcome" as the sun was setting golden behind the huge white dome. Then later, that night, the problems getting out of the city and to the airport (two of our group having been shot in the first black-white mixed carload). How I panicked, thinking of my pregnant wife and two young children back home, and would not help King carry his suitcases to the plane for fear of a bomb-plant. Cowardly I admitted, and shamed by it then because of the 'pact' that John Howard Griffin had told me that he and King and Dick Gregory made in an Atlanta hotel, "We must all *act as if we are already dead*, and then we will be *free* to do what we have to, without any fear or reservations."

Tom flinched, his face tightening at the mention of such suffering and injustice. Through his many writings, Tom was very active in the Peace Movement at the time — possibly the most informed, articulate, and influential person in the country speaking on this very serious but complex issue. He believed that all of us have a "duty to work for the total abolition of war." We must preach peace. Nonviolence needs to be understood not only as a spiritual way of life, but as "a practical method for peace" — and not left to be "mocked as an outlet for crackpots who want to make a show of themselves."

Tom was now becoming agitated as he spoke. He didn't want to identify with the sort of "false martyrs who glory in proving everyone else terribly and visibly wrong!" — objecting to the self-righteousness that so often infected protest groups.

Not too long before, Tom had been severely criticized in the Louisville newspapers for advising a conscientious objector to the Vietnam War; his counsel to the young man was simply "to follow the true dictates of your personal conscience" — which was interpreted by many as advocating 'draft-dodging'.

This gross misunderstanding, as well as many others, still deeply hurt Tom, and a frown creased the lines in his brow now as we talked about it there beside the lake.

And seeing Tom's expression darken, the light dimming in his eyes, I became agitated. Without thinking, I started to rail against the American Dream — my not being at home with that kind of naive romanticism.

"We need the rawmeat courage to face with honesty the *Holy Absurd!*" I declared half in jest, raising my fist, smiling, embarrassed by the sound of my rebel rhetoric.

And then I began telling him about my visit to a new shopping center in Louisville a few nights before. The memory of it now making me even more angry, making me stand up, talking loud, almost shouting. Describing to him a thousand people wandering with blind vacuous stares of boredom. Myself included. "With nothing better to do with our lives than *buy!* . . . Buy anything, but buy. Millions of 'things' stacked, spread on display to catch the eye, the tongue, the numbed brain of America's soulless vision!"

I was standing there flailing my arms, mouthing all this bad poetry, this confession of shame and self-hatred.

"What the damned rococo place needs is a heady depression! A wipeout to mausoleum! . . . Not a 'necessity' in the place. Only the whorecheap draw to mask! . . . the jangle dull glint of excess to hide."

Tom sat there, calm, patiently letting me spend my venom — waiting for the 'noise' to quit. Then he quietly picked up on my last word and continued, more solemn than usual, . . . telling me:

"Hide. —Yes, hide the noble utter nakedness of who we are . . . poor people on this planet, numbed by the shock of lacklove, the reality of loneliness. True solitude. We who sometimes cannot take the pierce, the stab, the *ask of creation* — the demand that we face our nakedness and celebrate it with life . . . the demand of *God-awe-full* courage, tight nerve, not to crack in the face of Abyss. Because there is no purchase-power to resist or avoid that 'standing your ground' (though sometimes with a flinch!) to open yourself to this reality of living — no gluttonous appetite satisfied to negate this core-element, definition-seed of 'who you are' as human.

"Lust to vomit is no ridding of love-hunger!"

Those last words Tom's affectionate mock-mimicry of my poetic stance of outrage. —Then continuing in a similar tone and choice of words:

"You and all the rest . . . me too, probably moreso . . . are going to have to give up on that spiritually bankrupt so-called American Dream. That man-alone-against-the-frontier-challenge-to-win. That competitive proof-of-manhood that depends upon dominion. That stand-off don't-touch lone silhouette atop a rock against the sky. That historical immortality of the hero as warrior and performance-champion who saves the wagontrain in a halo of the good white hat. That distorted version of self that replaces the true living of person!

"Be through with all that. Like *The Loneliness of the Long Distance Runner*, you don't want to beat anyone, you don't want to win. You don't want your sense of interior excellence based upon public approval.

"To hell with that death eat!"

Laughing — the last line a direct quote from one of my recent anger poems — Tom reminded me again that my imagined enemy-scapegoats were not America or capitalism or the unwashed masses, but *myself*, my response to the world: creation.

Then, with my youthful howl of protest muffled by his humbling composure, we settled back down to more important matters.

Tom closed his eyes, lay back with hands folded behind his head, facing the wide still sky . . . and began a spontaneous running inspired monologue that was truly the most enlightened reading of the spiritual life of modern man I shall ever have the privilege of experiencing. A sweeping verbal mural and insightful mosaic of bits and pieces of history, anthropology, theology, philosophy, psychology, and art . . . that was so orchestrated, with such fluid harmony (the improvisation of a jazz composition) that when finally come full circle and whole, complete — I was emptied and filled, awash and aglow with whatever truth was available to me at that

time. Mesmerized with the unity of everything, the *one* of it all . . .
it was then I was initiated into the *vision of poet*!

As the afternoon dimmed, and we got ready to go back to the
hermitage, I remember Tom turning a last time to look out over the
lake now lit golden in the setting sun, and saying: "You know, it
wasn't long ago that Joan Baez was here visiting, and sat down
there on the far end of the wall with the light full on her face and
shining her long hair. She brought her guitar with her, and sang
some songs. It was beautiful."

Then, turning back to me, he said: "Funny, but a long time ago,
when I first came here to Gethsemani, I said that this place is the
center of America. I had wondered then just what was holding the
country together . . . really what was keeping the whole universe
from cracking into pieces and falling apart. —It is places like this
monastery."

And placing his hand on my shoulder, he added, "I believed it
then, and I believe it now . . . even moreso."

———————◆———————

Monks Pond. Old Hermit. Hai!
The letters of those words forming on my tongue to sound in my
breathing as I stop to rest a half mile through the woods away from
the lake and now standing in tall waving winter grass all around me.

The sky is again clouded over gray and thickening with the
look of snow to come. I button my denim work-jacket against the
cold and pull the small hand-journal from my side pocket and toss
it to the ground in front of me as I drop to kneel with the heels of
my workboots a seat of sorts to rest while

> clean and white the wind
> opens the blank page notebook
> lying in the grass

ready for write and lines to Tom long gone now but with me still,
listening—

> strange
> that I should be here
> the eve of your 20th year
> into death

waiting for winter
and haiku
poems to appear
on my writing tablet

sitting
with sad mustache
to be iced
in December

my Zhivago white eyes
empty
with
light

I lay the pen across the scribbled words and put my hand palm down against the grass to feel the warm brown look of it. Then I press my spread fingers hard to the ground until I know that the red indentation will crisscross the skin when I raise my hand to touch my cheek. Do this . . . wait . . . and *be here.*

The walk from the lake has made my right foot ache. Even the heavy boots are not enough to support my mending bones. Twenty-three years now since I fell under the back wheels of a sand truck and lay in a hospital bed with a crushed foot. Two weeks there, not knowing that Tom was just a floor above me with his back in traction again. Both of us unawares of our shared solitude, finally belonging to the same community of 'providential pain'.

Until a week after, while I'm sweating away the summer day on frontporch with leg propped up in a cast and a big flatbed farmer truck pulls into my yard and out jumps Tom striding towards me yelling, "Cheer Up! Cheer Up!" — and holding a six-pack of Budweiser in each hand high above his head. A welcome sight, unexpected surprise for Sally and me: a generous gesture, warm friendly gift from Tom . . . he trying his best to ease the anxiety, lighten the load of our 'hurting situation' (the fear of my losing the foot, or not being able to walk again).

But even cold beer and Tom's healing laughter could do little to rouse me from my morphine stupor as I sat there sunken-eyed, junkie-pale and silent, unsmiling. A lucky break for him when the

visit cut short by the arrival of several seminarians from the college
— Tom bolting for the truck to avoid the 'recognition commotion'
among the students, and a big wave goodbye as his Brother driver
raised a cloud of gravel speeding away.

Remembering that now as I sit here waiting for the pain in my
foot to numb again. My stare into the past softened by a line of
white crossing my sight.

> how fleeting it was—
> that one snowflake through the grass
> this winter morning

Snowing again. Flurries falling slowly over the far fields. And
tilting my face back to feel the soft flakes brush breaking across
my cheeks, I squint my eyes to see the clouds open to a clear sky
above me.

> these snowflakes just now—
> a long time to be falling
> from the clear blue sky

Putting my notebook and pen in my jacket pocket, I push
myself back up and stand a moment looking into the distance I
must still cover to get back to the highway. A slight shiver hunches
my shoulders and I begin walking.

The dried leaves crunch beneath my boots as I step out of the
short stretch of woods and walk the last few yards through the
thick pasture grass before stopping at the edge of the highway —
ending the long hike from Monks Pond.

I look down the asphalt pavement rising away to curve south
into Marion County and the towns of New Hope, St. Francis, and
Loretto, then cross over and onto the narrow dirt road that leads a
mile or so through more woods to Tom's hermitage.

There is a wide iron gate here, locked and blocking anyone but
the monks' entry, and I stop again, leaning my crossed arms over
the top bar — just as I had done some twenty years before on May
6, 1968.

———————◆———————

Tom had written, requesting a ride to the Louisville airport for his trip west to Our Lady of the Redwoods Abbey in California, to return again, stopping at Christ in the Desert monastery in New Mexico — a brief journey in preparation for the longer one planned to the Far East in early September. So I went out to the Abbey the afternoon before and stayed in one of the small rooms at the guesthouse. Unable to sleep, I sat up almost all night, listening to the sounds (and silence) of the monastery from my open window, and writing little notebook poems in the dark:

> opening   onto rooftops
> the upstairs window
> (the mystery of distance in the whistles)

> There!   the side of the church!
> the still white glow of stone
> shining into the night

> head back
> arms spread
> my (nailed by the moon
>   held by its light) face
> crucified in whiteness

The next morning, at 6:00 AM, just as we had scheduled, I was standing at the gate, looking up the dirt road. Waiting.

And then he came. Rising from beyond the crest of the hill. His head, then body, up on over, now down the road, out of the darkness . . . first waving. Then calling, laughing, hello-ing my name on the air, "Ron!" — a voiced embrace out of the dawn silence.

And watching him come striding the long road towards me, I pulled my notebook from my coat pocket and began scribbling

> the bells ringing you
> out of the mist   Tom Merton
> walking the dirt road
> at 6:00 AM   towards me

> the morning light lifting
> the sky behind you

black black you come
down the road black
your head now shoulders now
all of you   Tom Merton
coming towards me
black

this good May morning
1968

The scrawled words on the page closed into the notebook stuffed back into my pocket as I reached over the gate to clasp his hand with "Hello . . . yes . . . good . . . get going, eh?"

Tom unlocked and relocked the wide swinging gate and we got into the car and took off, driving that two-laned strip of asphalt through and past the monastery grounds. We began talking about the trip, both of us excited by the adventure of it and the rush of just the *moving* itself.

Tom had gotten me interested in photography not long before, and we kept slowing down and gawking out the window, pointing to objects and scenes that we'd like to photograph if we had the time. Especially the rundown wooden shacks and abandoned clapboard lean-to, weathered-board barns, weeds growing out of rusting old autos, broken bottles glinting in the sun.

We talked about doing motion pictures when he got back, both of us eager to give it a try, see what we could say.

"We'll call our first film 'Cold Beer Confession at Culvertown'," I said as we turned right onto Highway 31–E . . . "the small tavern where I used to stop and down a few before heading for Gethsemani to whisper my evil-doings into some poor monk's warming ear."

Tom now wide-awake laughing with energy and enthusiasm of things behind, things ahead, as I took the Bardstown bypass and cut west along the road towards Bernheim Forest and on past till we reached the turnpike (I-65) that would speed us into Louisville.

I could feel our bodies radiating light as we rode. All at once I found myself beating the steering wheel with my palms, anxious to tell Tom my thoughts since our last get-together a few weeks before . . . of that daylong talk by the lake and some of what I now understood him to be saying then — what he had set free in me that Monks Pond sermon-in-the-sun picnic. "Finally, after all these years, after some sort of purgative wash, some Seven Storey Mountain climb, eh Tom — I'm *free*!"

Shouting this to Tom in the frontseat of the car as we weaved our way through the turnpike traffic. "Free of *Them*! . . . whoever the hell *they* ever were. —Those damned people whom I've been telling myself were killing me. My persecutors, my prosecutors. The cause of all my tangles and lacklove. Strangling my true-blue creative person by not 'understanding' me. By their insensitivity, their ignorance, their hate and violence . . . . But, it's just the opposite! I've been killing myself for years. . . . And this morning, this very moment — I call off my lifelong suicide!"

Tom was rocking in his seat with choking laughs, clapping his hands in applause as I ended my pronounced breakthru to wisdom, my belated, long-a-coming farewell to spiritual adolescence.

"Satori! Satori!" he shouted. —"And right in the middle of Highway 65 at that. . . . If I had my cereal bowl, I'd be Zen Master and crack you over the head with it," laughing.

But I was wound up and went on, pounding my fist on the dashboard: "A brief history of my life up to this moment — *Vanity*!"

Rolling his window down, Tom yelled, "Air! I need air!"

"But maybe there's still time to unchisel that script from my cold stone grave lay. A new day, a new week — a new life, always, each moment," I came back with raised voice, continuing my 'break-thru' moving testimonial. "And now, at long last, I do not hate anyone, anything. This land where my body breathes, this place called America — each stumbling bum one of us, man and woman falling flat a failure in midstretch — I love too.

"I am a super-patriot of Creation!"

Both of us now laughing as Tom says, "Pull over at the next service station. I want to wash out my ears."

And on into Louisville.

———◆———

It is almost noon now, my arms still resting on the iron bar atop the wide gate that blocks entry to the narrow dirt road that winds its way a mile or so through the woods to Tom's hermitage . . . the memory of that special day in May some twenty years ago slowly fading, but not quite the end of it.

I reach down into the side pocket of my jacket, pull out my notebook and remove the marker stuck between the pages. Another postcard from Tom, this one from San Francisco and post-marked May 6, 1968, the same day he left for his trip west. The picture side is an ordinary tourist photo of the Golden Gate Bridge, and I smile thinking of him just grabbing it from a rack without looking as he rushed through the airport.

I turn the card over and look at Tom's hurried scribble (in green ink), a short note written on the run:

> *Dear Ron.*
>
> *Great flight out. Some calligraphies in those deserts!! Marvelous & unequaled. Could fly over them all day. On to mtns in a few minutes.*
>
> > *Tom*

Again his tight script hard to decipher. On to *mtns* (mountains)? Oh well — what's really important: Tom's painter-poet eye to the natural 'Zen Signatures' in the landscape seen from God's heaven-high view . . . the vision-light always on!

The card back in the notebook, I climb over the chest-high gate and step down just as a deep "Hello there" turns my eyes to a Brother's arm waving welcome

> on his high tractor
> riding the winter highway—
> monk in a white cowl

I raise my arm, "Hai!" (a Japanese greeting: *Yes*), and turn walk-ing up the road towards Tom's hermitage. Two narrow dirt ruts are worn deep by the monastery trucks and my hard bootsoles pinch the pebbles thrown up on the high strip running between them. The road splits into a Y ahead of me and I take the bend to the left and keep walking until a path through the brush opens on the right, and a few steps farther I'm approaching a clearing that widens into a stretch of grassland spreading all the way to a line of

GOLDEN GATE BRIDGE
This is the world's tallest and largest single span suspension bridge. It was built at a cost of $35,500,-000 and crosses the historic Golden Gate of San Francisco. Two main cables towers 746 ft. tall support 36½ inch master cables from which is suspended a 90 ft. wide 6 lane traffic deck and two pedestrian walks, 266 feet above San Francisco Bay.

Dist. by Smith News Co., 460 Ninth St., San Francisco, Calif. ....

POST CARD

Dear Ron.
Great flight out. Some
calligraphies in those
deserts!! Marvelous +
unequalled. Could fly
over them all day.
On to mine in a few
minutes. Tom

Prof. Ron Seitz
Bellarmine College
2000 Norris Pl.
Louisville, Ky
40205

pine trees some fifty yards in the distance. There, at the foot of those trees, I can see a small white cinderblock hut, Tom's place — the hermitage that the monastery built for him in 1961 and which he visited whenever possible, but the 'home' that he had to wait until 1965 to live in full-time.

As I walk closer I can see firewood chopped and stacked on the concrete floor of the full-length roofed frontporch. The panes of the large front window reflect a square of sunlight as the clouds part and close again before I reach the tall wooden cross carved from two thin tree trunks standing a few feet to the left of the porch. A large iron wagon wheel leans rusting against the base of the cross.

I stop now and, with one knee touching the ground, I wrap my right hand around the flat rim of the wheel. I hold it there, pressing tightly, until I feel the cold from deep inside the iron shoot through my wrist and fill my arm: homage to this special place of prayer that was Tom's.

It doesn't matter that one of the monks knocked down the original cross with his tractor, then cut the wood for kindling — that this is a replacement, and smaller. I look up to the two trees crossed against the sky now filled with falling flakes of snow thinly white-ing the rough wooden arms held hard against the cold . . . and know, in some small way, the spirit Tom shared in this "from-all-time selected spot of creation."

Thomas Merton's hermitage in the monastery woods at the Abbey.

Cross made from windfalls outside Merton's hermitage in Abbey woods.

With the steady falling windless snow wetting my upturned face, "All will be well, and all will be well" . . . *resurrection*

Here
Now

rest, open
in clear light
and wait

to be empty

——

even as you look
I disappear

My body
becoming Spirit

leaves Nothing
and skeleton

———◆———

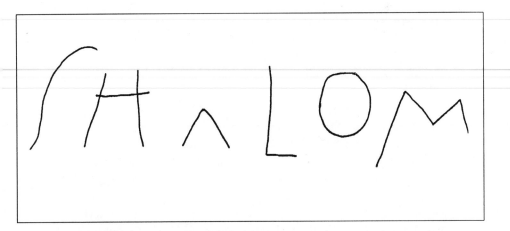

The word on a square of brown wood, eye level, to the right of the door and entry to the hermitage of Thomas Merton.

"Peace" . . . returning the welcome — then trace the crooked letters on a page torn from my notebook.

I knock my knuckles on the wood frame. No answer.

> Lift the bar from your door
> And let Basho in
>
> He brings with him
> The winter moon
> And just maybe
> A bottle

I try the doorknob. Locked.

> Might I rent your rock
> Your tiny hut
> To love from
>
> Speechless

No one home.

But the hermitage is supposed to be empty; I have made arrangements at the monastery to spend the afternoon here. A key has been provided.

The door pushes open and I step in out of the light to stand in a large room dark with shadows — the front study, extending the entire width of the hut and originally built for small conferences.

Closing the door behind me, I wait a few moments as my eyes adjust to the objects in the room taking on light.

The shine of smooth wood turns my head to the right and the well-worn top of the handmade Victor Hammer desk: Tom's workplace. It is not large (three by five feet of writing surface), with a desk lamp at the rear and a wind-up clock to one side. Now clean of Tom's typewriter, working papers, and books — its small wooden chair empty, the back legs just touching the large Indian rug between the desk and stone fireplace in the wall directly behind it.

Unbuttoning my jacket I remember the three wooden peg clothes-hangers behind me on the left wall as you enter. I turn with my jacket in hand and stop. There is nothing on the bare hangers, but

> how silent this light
> caught cold in his empty cowl—
> room of the dead monk

Merton's rocking chair at his hermitage.

an image haunting my memory and . . . I drop the jacket atop a small lift-top desk just inside the door.

It is not too cold in the hermitage now but, if I'm going to spend several hours here, the first thing to do is make the place comfortable. And that means a trip back out to the frontporch for an armful of logs to get the fire going. Then a pot of water boiling on the stove for tea. Not to mention positioning the small rocking chair just right in front of the fireplace when the wood is flaming the room warm with light. —Much as it was almost thirty years ago, when . . . .

———◆———

It was my first visit to the hermitage sometime in 1961 . . . an ecumenical gathering of Protestant and Jewish theologians not long before the Second Vatican Council 'shake-up' in the Catholic Church. Tom sitting in his rocker chair, back to the fire and welcoming the circle of visitors with open arms and eyes for a friendly dialogue in the newly built 'conference center'.

Patient, relaxed, always smiling, Tom listened to the interchange of ideas and convoluted language that seemed only to con-

fuse the issues as the educated 'thinkers' voiced their solemn specu-
lations.

"Give me an image! An image!" he would finally say as his great
gift of poetic intuition pierced the heart of each apparently obscure
issue with such wise simplicity that I would grin a silent *Yes, yes!*

An unspeaking spectator and audience — who also served as
filler of coffee mugs, log-bearer, and stoker of the fire — I sat back
off in a corner of the room, nodding my assent to point after point
that Tom made with his crackling intelligence, his imaginative rea-
soning.

It was winter and cold that day too, with flits of snow blowing
the other side of the large front window. And I remember writing
Tom a short note the next day about the Zen truth of that meeting
— a little poem inspired by the juxtaposition of his humble smile
with

> maybe the year's last—
> that snowflake past the window
> quickly melting now

behind him as he hit home with raised finger the pulse of what we
were all seeking . . . that 'given' image fusing all of the ideas
bandied about that day.

A hut haiku long lost in laughter now these many years.

———————◆———————

With two armloads of wood carried in from the cold frontporch
and stacked beside the fireplace now, I feel warm again, even without my jacket. Sitting in the rocker I take off my heavy Alpine
boots. My thick hunting socks are soft and feel good as I stand and
step off the rug onto the smooth concrete floor.

I .want to take time to walk around the hermitage and see if
things have changed much since my last visit — get to *know it*
again. Besides this large front room, there are two rooms in the
rear: one a kitchen, the other a bedroom (both small). And off to
the side of these, on the left, is a chapel and a bathroom (again,
both small) — these rooms built later and much-needed additions.
Especially the indoor toilet.

The original hermitage had an outhouse a short distance away
towards the woods. And in one of his journals, Tom tells us about

his adventurous narrow escapes from a snake who used to inhabit the warm confines of that privy. He would stand a few feet back, outside the door, and, before entering, yell, "Are you in there, you bastard?" (A one-line Zen poem really, that I took the liberty of titling "Snake in The Outhouse," and which I silenced a much too formal poetry reading with one night.)

Thinking of this I remember Tom telling me that neither of us could ever write haiku poems, really good 'true' ones, because "After all, we're not Eastern now, are we? I mean, our entire consciousness, our way of living, has been formed here in the West. And that's something you just can't change overnight, if ever. No matter how much reading or Zen exercises we practice, eh."

Probably right, no doubt, I tell myself as I walk over to the desk . . . but I keep writing them anyway.

With light filling the wide window I pull out the small wooden chair and sit at Tom's workplace, opening my notebook, and look out over the spread of pasture now snow-covered and on to the bottom land to the distant woodland hills south — enjoying the same beautiful view of the monastery landscape changing with the seasons that Tom did as he wrote.

View out front window from Merton's desk at his hermitage.

Seeing my reflection in the glass iced at the bottom outside, I pick up my pen, bend to the empty page, and

> in the room his breath
> steaming up the window pane—
> outside, stars of frost

The look of the looped letters black on the white paper raises my eyes to the wall near the door — the long scroll with black ink Japanese calligraphy that D. T. Suzuki sent Tom . . . "No. Don't know what it says, but no matter — beautiful anyway, eh?" he had told me . . . a carved wooden crucifix now where it hung.

Turning to the lattices on the wall behind me . . . not there either. An ikon and stringbead tapestry.

> Winter brings a chill
> on afternoons not yet dark—
> the empty fireplace

. . . a feeling of the traces of Tom's presence slowly going. Gone.

But not our love of Chuang-Tzu, Han-shan, Huang Po — all of those beautiful Zen Masters, Holy Fools, *wu-wei* followers of the trackless Tao! . . . the Herakleitos waters that Tom had me wade in when I came to him wanting desperately to understand and appreciate and experience, to *know* the true reality, the *mystery of Christ*. Because, I told him,, in all honesty the person of Jesus as an historical figure, as a 'manifestation of the Divine', an avatar or whathaveyou . . . had not been the center of my conscious spiritual life. Telling him that, for me, it was not an honest, natural, spontaneous act to think of or voice the name of Jesus or Christ. —My *Cold Night of the Soul* . . . what was that about?

And Tom not answering my anxious querying but just hinting that it seems that I just might be looking for some "wrong indication" or "subjective response" that "flirts with *facting* the Incarnation!" . . . that possibly my 'Christian vocation' is never to recognize the name of Jesus — only to realize the "eternal Presence in absence, the *void of recognition!*" . . . that possibly my 'conversion' (so-called) is not becoming other than this, but a deepening of it — "the living question that is your life!"

"Who is the Christ who shows you his faceless face?" a big question, Tom had said. "But first, find your own original face before you were born. Do that . . . and there's not even one face — that or thou."

The stones of the fireplace behind me have drawn to darkness the light reflecting my face in the glass, and no one now looks out the window to see the snow slowly descending upon the rolling bottomland and blanking white the distant tree-lined hills.

I reach over and place the palm of my left hand flat upon the edge of the desk . . . where twenty-five years ago the manuscript of my first novel lay when I came out to the hermitage after a letter from Tom suggested we get together and talk about it.

Dear Ron

Dan reminded me last evening that you were still waiting for some reaction on my part to your story of "Grampaw Snow." I like it very much. It is very alive. I think you have really got something there, and I wish you all success with it. Certainly you will find someone to print it. . . . Dan said something about you applying for a fellowship. I do not know if I got it straight, but if you need a recommendation from me, I give it. On the basis of your book I think you ought to have support and encouragement in developing your talent and your work.

> *Blessings, and best wishes . . .*
> *Cordially yours in Christ,*
> *Fr. Louis*

A most formal, cordial letter, signed Fr. Louis rather than the friend "Tom" because very early in our relationship, and the both of us uncomfortable about the "fellowship thing" and our coming meeting as "novice writer circle-dancing with established critic," as he later put it.

The novel, *Somewhere the Other Side* (the second half, *Winter of the Grandpa Snow*, referred to in Tom's letter), was an autobiographical account of a 'religious crisis and resulting breakdown' in my twelfth year. A very self-conscious work, labored and re-written completely some fourteen times — this fact bemoaned by Tom, "You're squeezing all the life out of it. Stop, let it go! . . . Sit on the thing till someone comes, asks to publish." Advice accepted and to this day still held in trust, though years ago the wait began to 'long' a bit thin. But of that, another time. . . .

———◆———

"What do you think of it?"—jabbing my finger against the black cover of the manuscript.

Tom was bent over putting more wood on the fire, his back to me. And when he straightened up and turned around, my rigid stance and stare seemed to surprise him.

"Oh, your book," he grinned, raising a hand towards it.

"Did you read it?"

"Sure. Sure I did. . . .Whatja think, I'd be like your Zen Master?"—referring to my recent poem,

Decision

the night the   Master
burned a statue of   Buddha
to keep warm

must have been a   cold one

Laughing, then waiting a few seconds as he saw me looking down at the floor.

"Dan said you thought it was funny. That you laughed all the way through."

"Oh, not that way 'funny'. . . I meant that it was right, you had got things so true . . . It lives! It really does. —A moving thing. I mean it. . . . Just like I said in the letter."

Embarrassed somewhat now at the look of my hurt, Tom went on to tell me that he was laughing at the parts of the book that made him see exactly how it was with "the Catholic thing when you're just a child — how truly *terrible* some of that kind of stuff you get from certain priests and nuns can be". . . even if they don't even have a hint of what they are saying or doing.

Sure, he could even smile now at how I had got it "right on the nose" in the book — but it must have been some kind of hell for me while it was going on. He knew that. . . . You bet.

"And writing about it didn't work either," I told him. "Didn't get rid of it. . . . I'm still angry and blaming people for what they did to me — the *Church*, that is."

Tom stood there looking at me, listening patiently while I went on raving in anger, damning this and that to hell and back. Then, in a voice of caring and true sympathy, said softly, "You got hurt, Ron, no doubt about it. And deeply, to be sure. In the worst way — by being disappointed, possibly even betrayed, by someone or something you sincerely loved and trusted and needed. . . . your so-called 'Church', your religion. Which is no small matter. —Probably the most important thing in your life then."

He reached down and grabbed the poker leaning against the fireplace and turned back to the fire, rolling the new logs onto the pile of glowing ashes now flitting sparks up the chimney and *flepping* small flames curling the bark in *sphits* and crackles.

"But you must know one thing, Ron . . .and it's most important. —The true Church is not that institution, not that hierarchy, not that formal organization which so hurt you as a child and which is now the target of your rage . . .The true Church is a living Community of Love!

"Now you take what you want and what you need and what is good from that other so-called 'Church'. . . and then you go on and live your life in joy."

But the full import of what Tom had said was smothered by my anger. I went on to tell him about my near nervous breakdown, the psychiatrists, thoughts about suicide . . . "all of that sensitive bullcrap," punching my finger against the manuscript again. "You're a convert. Didn't have to go through all that stuff. John Howard, convert! Bob Lax, convert! The Maritains, converts! Greene, Waugh, even Eliot a convert of sorts. Everybody I know who is big on Christianity, Catholicism, seems to be a convert! You're all lucky about that, I can tell you."

Tom was still looking.into the fire, his back to me, and I could hear my voice loud and echoing in the small room, the last words seeming to hang high up in the corners of the ceiling.

"Yeah, you might have something there, could be right about that . . . but then again, maybe not," Tom said calmly as he turned to again face me. "Guilty . . . possibly," now smiling, holding his palms out and up.

There was a moment of silence between us. I felt embarrassed, ashamed.

"But Ron, you took all of that pain and suffering and transformed it into beauty. That's what poetry's all about, eh? . . . An artist responds to something that is not only true, but honestly put. —And my response to good art, a poem is almost always a smile, and manytimes laughter! Even if the stuff is really tragic and you see just how awful things can get sometimes. . . . You know, you smile by saying to the poet or whoever, You bet! —It's how I say I'm enjoying it. Know what I mean?"

"Yeah." I had to agree. Telling him that I laughed all the way through Sartre's *Nausea*, and Beckett's plays, and almost everything that Kafka wrote.

"Sure. . . . Joy there in the beauty of the truth of it. . . . The stuff of Hell itself sometimes. What a world without God really is! . . . Those people put a thumb to the pulse, touch the horrible heart of it all. They really do," Tom went on.

Then pausing, to look me straight on, "And I thank every one of those poor hurting artist-bastards, Van Gogh and Rimbaud and the rest, for it . . . their unsidedown twisted blessing-curse of the poet's eye."

Tom was right about all this. He knew directly and concretely from the experience of the reading of Joyce and finding poetry, the seeds of his own conversion, in the painful curse of *Ulysses* upon Catholicism — realizing the power of a particular Religion and Church that could generate such a passionate condemnation from so great an artist's soul.

Suddenly I realized that I was looking into Tom's eyes and, somehow, without my noticing the change . . . he had turned the entire thing around and we were both smiling now.

"Tell you what," he said, trying to hold back laughing ". . . how about doing us both some good by reading a piece of that pain . . . the opening section. You know, the brother — really you, three years older, fifteen—writing the letter home."

I was objecting, oh no, that's not the hurting — just some of the literary parts. But he had me laughing now too as he walked over, picked up the manuscript off the desk and rolled the pages back to "Here. This part . . . go ahead," stepping back again to sit down in his rocking chair, "and do your Dylan Thomas impersonation too, okay?"

I didn't know why (and still don't), but he was right. It was the thing to do then.

So, clearing my throat, still embarrassed, I glanced up at him rocking gently back and forth in front of the fire, the flicker of flames lighting the left side of his face off and on . . . hesitated a moment, then began.

Let me tell you of Church in the winking gray mornings of sleepy
    schoolwalks along damp brickstreets through our neighbor-
    hood—
Kicking a rock past all the white wooden cottages with black iron
    fences and creaking gates by the rolling sidewalk,
we felt the shadowy haze of early dawn cool our faces and send lonely
    chills down our backs,
trailed up the long steep alleyhill past the garbage cans spilling over
    with dangling rope and twisted shoes,
yae-yaeed the barking dogs who leaped against the backfences baring
    their teeth to us,
rounded corners, crossed alleys, and cut down streets to make our
    way to the red brick church standing tall against the cloudy sky,
the white tower with bell hanging seen blocks away
(we hoping it wouldn't ring before we climbed the steps leading to
    the big heavy doors that would squeak at the wide swinging and
    twist of iron handles cold in our hands)—
Tossle-capped, corduroyed, skinned-shoeed schoolboys leaning
    forward with books carried tiredly under our arms—

The Church inside was high and pillared with a coldness hanging up
    by the ceiling,
the altar far away and solemn with flickering candles glowing the
    little blue and red bulbs,
the statues looking dry and dusty with the shine of creases and folds
    in the draping gowns they wore
(faces forever peaceful and serene as they looked down at us),
the confessional bare and cold-looking
(holding so much dread and mystery behind the hanging purple
    drape in front,
the light not burning and the booth empty inside)—
All of it gray and sleepy in the yellow-lighted earlymorning church
    with priest up on the altar in black vestments swishing around
    with cape flying out on a spin and raising of the hand to bless us,
the altarboys kneeling there wiggling shoesoles at the congregation
    behind them—

And Sister would flick her clean nail over the metal piece in her hand
    that sent a click echoing over the church,
a hollow clear sound that rung its way around the columns and up
    the stained glass windows to the plaster walls and ceiling painted
    in gold designs
(now dirty from years of hanging there above heads listening to the
    lonely ring of altar bells),
and we would genuflect to the hard marble aisle (specks of gold in
    the white graying,
under scuffle of old lady shoes every Saturday night for confession
    lines and six o'clock penances)—

O, all this and more, always—
A CHILD'S CHURCH AGO

The echo of the rhythm and roll of language still sounded
inside me as the room (having dropped away in the reading) slowly
came back — my whole body enveloped in the music of words
voiced from my mouth conducted by the memory of Dylan
Thomas singing my ear — as I looked up to see Tom sitting there a
few feet away, his eyes wide and receptive now locked to mine.

"Yeah!. . .Right!" he stood, clapping his hands, a big grin pushing his cheeks up shining. "Aloud! you got to read it aloud," he
almost shouted. "The only way. Hear the words! . . . —Always the
sure sign of a good poem: your lips start moving when you see the
words on the page. To sound them inside you. . . pure joy!"

Still holding the book, I could feel my face warming red.

"when memory thinks the words aloud: soliloquy—
language in sound, for the ear
    & eye enough to watch the waves of music now"

I said as a solemn pronouncement, closing the issue.

"Okay. Your round, your round," Tom holding up his arms in a
gesture of surrender.

"As a friend of mine once said, 'when you stop, don't stop to
think of words, but to see the picture better'. . . Yes!" — accepting
his challenge.

"*The Unspeakable Visions of the Individual!*. . .ol' Jacko Keroway,
eh," Tom laughed. "—You know he was supposed to stop by and
spend a few days out here . . . what Lax told me anyway."

"He could sure use it. —I told you I saw him standing out front
of City Lights bookstore, 1960, in disguise," shaking my head.

"That's when he was living his *Big Sur* book. He mentions that night on the first page . . . Can't help it, I just like the guy."

"Sure. . . . 'Learn the language, then forget it'. . . he (among others) said that too about writing."

"Poetry is your natural speech . . . everything else is distorted. —Think that's mine," I said, laughing.

"Enough! Beginning to sound like a seminar on poetics . . . *Ta dah* — back to the Academy," Tom pointing at me.

"Right. —Let my voice be the presence of silence, not the absence of noise," I apologized, with open palms extended.

"Anyway, I'm not going to read or write anything but poetry for the next ten years! . . . Enough of this running off at the mouth about anything and everything every five minutes — writing essays and articles for newspapers, magazines, this group that group. Time to call a halt." Tom chopped the air with a stiff hand.

I looked at him, knowing that he really meant what he said, but aware also that tomorrow he'd be back at it again . . . because someone had to speak out, someone who had something to say.

"Anyway, what I really wanted to tell you, Ron, is that you are a poet . . . and everything you write will be poetry. And you're always going to have to sit on it! — even in your so-called 'fiction' or whatever kind of prose work . . . to keep the poems from bulging the surface, bursting out in music all over the place," pausing, "or if not music, some tight stacked image of a Cezanne canvas. That's another approach."

"And the two together is what has to happen in haiku," I interrupted, trying to keep up but not following what Tom was after here.

"What happened again and again in your novel there," Tom pointing to the manuscript still in my hands, "find that other place where your brother is describing how he thought Christ really looked at the crucifixion . . . not as both of you had to see him in your church — one of those pretty plaster Jesus-hurting all weepy on the Cross — the kind of dimestore awful art they call 'religious'. Whew! we've even got some of the stuff here at the Abbey — should be stripped from the walls."

I knew what he was referring to in the book and found the page while he was still talking. "You mean this part."

"Not exactly Cézanne, that . . . more like the Spanish El Greco or one of those bent mystic-artists who really twisted Jesus to the wood there," Tom said in a quick laugh.

"Yeah, maybe," I said, again uncomfortable.

"Go on, read that. See what I mean about your writing."

"Naw. . . not me. You can read it if you want to—and I'll sit down and listen this time," handing him the open manuscript.

"Okay. Not my stuff, so might not do what you had in mind. . . . No time to be shy. After all, it's *my* house," grinning.

I walked around Tom and sat in his rocker, crossing my legs and laying my head back against the wood, waiting for him to begin.

"Not great poetry, but not the kind of stuff you find in the mouth of a twelve-year old boy telling a story either." And then he was reading:

> the Cross brown rough, gaping holes
>   in splintered wood
> put together lopsided, thrown into the
>   ground leaning
> Jesus hanging with feet piled arched and
>   toes spread cramped running thin blood
>   around a black metal nail shining
>   into mushed flesh swelled over bones
>   bared and broken
> scrawny pale legs bent out to popping knee-
>   bones
> jagged spear holes in calves bruised purple,
>   punctured muscle
> hip bones thrust out aching against the
>   white cloth hanging
> the chill shiver of bowel ache
> chestcage expanded to rib bones pushing
>   white beneath thin olive-colored skin
>   shining bloodsweat
> a sharp quiver of pain stabbing the heart
> hollows of underarms deep and hairless,
>   the weight pulling wrists tight, elbows
>   locked in a bending curve
> hands chewed palms, the nails splitting
>   grinding, the entire body pulling
> fingers pointed upward stretched, white
>   boney joints reaching
> head hung limp against the collarbone broken
> hair strung wet down the bulge of neckbone
>   in back

corners of the mouth white with slime sticky
    and drying
lips rolled out in blubber and tongue lolled
    thick between teeth protruding too big
haze of bloodsweat in the cheek hollows
wet eye sockets shining purple
a crown of tangled thorns piled high bubbling
    blood
now slobber oozed up from hollow heaving and
    coughed gurgles in the chest
the chaag sound of nervous vomit raised
    in the throat
a loud throb in the head forcing lids open
    to popeyes and a cloudy film seeing
    glazed lopsided dark ground with a
    blur of upturned woman's face in black
    shawl
everything tired
slow
way down   faraway
halfreal
now slee py
fa   ding into dark
m o v i n g   slow ly
w a v i n g   gray
go i n g   black
ech o e s   m o v i n g
d u l l   sou nds   wwwhhhhrrrr i n g
set tling
brea th i n g
eeeeeeeeeeeeeehhhhhhhhhhhhhhh
c l o s e

Silence.

Tom's mouth had closed upon the last word as that word had closed the vision as written.

His voice soft on the air, speaking slowly — its kindness — had stilled me.

He had read words written by a twenty-three-year old man, someone much younger than his years — a person who sat there now with all of his embarrassment and shame washed into quiet peace. It no longer mattered that, five years later, hearing my words read back to me revealed just how poor the writing had been. Tom's gift was to make my work more than it was.

"Tried something there at the end — make language do something more than it can with sound and image — by playing around with typography. What cummings did a long time ago, and maybe a little of what Lax and others are about now in their poetry. . . . Don't know if it works here, but an okay go at it," Tom said, handing me the manuscript.

"Yeah, I know. . . ."

But before I could finish, Tom was walking to the door with, "Need some more wood." Opening it and, "Come on, get some fresh air and gimme a hand."

I put the manuscript on the desk and followed him out into a rush of cold air swirling snow onto the frontporch, piling thin lines of white atop the dark bark of the stacked logs there.

"But you're still in the same trap as what you're revolting against," Tom said, still talking about my piece he had just read. "Your description of the Crucifixion is a more realistic one, to be sure, than most of the so-called 'traditional' images which are almost sticky with sentimentality. But, both sides are looking at Christ's suffering there on the Cross in a literal sense . . . that is, the awful physical pain endured (and it *was* that too, you bet). But the real hurt, the infinite anguish of Jesus was that the people did not know (in the true spiritual sense of that word) him . . . which means, of course, a rejection of who he was — which was, in reality, a refusal of love!"

Tom was just standing there, not moving . . . looking at me. The blowing snow stuck to the side of his shirt and wet his cheek as he talked, "Can you think of a greater sin, or tragedy, or terrible *loss* that could happen to us?"

Tom had spoken each word of his last statement with such intensity, separating each syllable with held breath.

"Well, all this so obvious, I know. Sorry," he said as he turned to pick up a log. "I know you're.teaching theology at the college and you've read Bultmann and those other guys on this . . . but none of all that speculation (which is a good thing and all) is worth anything unless it is a *lived* theology. —You know, just as we agreed after that first meeting out here with that group of theologians."

"But that's what I thought I was saying in my book," I said as Tom turned around with the ends of a log cupped in both hands, "the reason I turned away from organized or institutionalized or whatever religion . . .what the first half is about, the "Child's Church Ago" section . . . to what some might call 'nature religion' or the worship of esthetics — what you find in the second half of the book, the ".Winter of the Grandpa Snow" section.

"What you see out there," I said, raising my arm in a wide sweep of all that land and woods and sky filled with falling snow before our eyes now looking out into the flakes white-ing the stretch of valley to the low foothills rising beyond the monastery in the dimming distance.

We both stood there a few moments, our stares into that 'other church' finally blanked by snow sticking our eyelids.

"Yes, what you say about that is true and beautiful . . . but it's not a case of either/or, this/that — but *both*." He turned towards the door. "The two are not at odds, are not mutually exclusive. . . . but *one*. —I know, believe me. Living out here has taught me that, if anything."

The door closed behind Tom and I was left standing alone on the porch. I could feel the snow sticking to the back of my shirt and see the fire inside flaming light through the window. The words "Somewhere the Other Side" moved my lips silently. . . and maybe, for the first time, I began to understand the title of my book.

The fingers of my left hand are still spread flat against the wood of Tom's desk, still pressing the long gone but remembered cover of my first novel. Lifting my arm now I see the moist palm print begin to fade, just as the vision of that years-ago experience with Tom and the book does. I push the chair back, stand and stretch my legs, walk around the room once before bending in front of the fire-place and striking a match across the stone and lighting the stuffed paper under the kindling under the logs.

Alone now in the hermitage with the fire burning brightly, I sit in Tom's rocking chair with a small blanket across my knees. The room is still cold. Sat at the desk too long before lighting the logs. —Remembering can do that . . . take you away for a long time. Time enough to chill you but, as now, time enough to warm you too. All depends upon what special memory unreels the vision of Tom behind my eyes. Imagining a day when

he   at the hermitage
in solitary rite the same moment
of my write

sitting his rocker before the fire
unfolding this paper with fingers
flickered by flame

heat eating the page edge
wrinkly crisping gray to black
a light ash float up the chimney
out to unvoiced words wavering
syllable by syllable on the still air
printing darkness hard to trees
beneath a dome freeze December sky
roofing silent in snow
those chalice'd high hands
warming the monastery
Whole Earth's Eucharist

—What I had requested of Tom when we first met . . . that he burn
any and all letters I would write him — explaining that I type on
long endless rolls of teletype paper with a carbon copy. . . . that
most of my writing to him would include very personal material,
the copy of which I would save in my own private files (so as not to
clutter his), to be made public later if worthwhile or necessary. —
And, as much as I can tell, Tom honored this request, and there are
no long coiling yellow jagged-end sheets of worded paper from me
anywhere in *The Collected Correspondence of Thomas Merton* housed
in some University library . . . but, to be sure, still around and
stuffed in a metal cabinet drawer in the corner of my basement
writing cell, waiting a distant day for other eyes "to world them."

Sliding the rocker closer to the fire, I pick up the notebook
from my lap and begin turning the pages covered with my hurried
hand-scrawl since early morning. Tongue-wet finger-flipping the
thin paper sheets until I come to the last entry inked at the desk
less than an hour ago . . . the beginning of another remembrance

A day in that last year, 1968, the second week
in February, a Friday it seems. . . .

Tom had permission from the Abbot to visit Louisville.

The day's planned schedule was to begin with me arriving at the hermitage at dawn, around seven o'clock. A matter of Tom clearing up some appointments with a few doctors, a meeting with the lawyer handling his Legacy Trust, then on to the Merton Studies Center at Bellarmine College to check a few details concerning his manuscript collection there. Afterwards, fulfilling Tom's wish "to make a full day of it" — visits with a few friends, lunch with J. Laughlin, his publisher at New Directions who had come down from New York, and finally, if everything worked out, dinner and a chance to hear some good jazz at a riverfront club down on Washington Street.

So a fog-shrouded winding drive up that deep-rutted dirt road in my big blue '66 Chevy Wagon, to roll bouncing through the grass and park alongside the hut and hear (while still in the car, windows up and doors closed to the cold) the sound of the Beatles blaring on Tom's recently borrowed phonograph. Then the music changing to Bob Dylan as I stepped up onto the front porch — Dylan whine-bending folk-blues notes, his voice and mouth harp blending one into the other, both at full volume.

At that time Tom was very enthusiastic about the songs and music of Dylan and the Beatles, and many others, including Joan Baez — for a special reason. Now that he had some of their records, he insisted on playing them for me — all the time pointing out the importance of their work as an "authentic expression of American art for our time." I once mentioned that the Beatles were from England, a fact that Tom impatiently disregarded as my "missing the point." He was so excited about this new youth expression and "much-alive counter-culture" that he planned to do a book about it, as well as "an entire history of Black Blues" — a project that sent me to all the music libraries in Louisville for a month — still another and another of his ever-growing list of diverse interests.

I was about to pound my fist on the outside screen door just as the solid inner door swung open with Tom singing, "They'll stone ya when you're there all alone" — laughing, grabbing my hand and pulling me inside with, "Everybody must get stoned!"

"Hey, how come you're not up, raring to go? Why so sleepy?" . . . my words mouthed mute into the wall of music.

"Sounds great, eh? Had anything to eat yet? 'They'll stone ya at the breakfast table' . . . . Come on, sit down a minute and listen. This is the new American poetry! —No kidding, it's that important!"

"You just said that last week about Lenny Bruce . . . that he was America's greatest living poet. Lot of great bards around, eh?"

In his unbounded enthusiasm he left me standing there and went into the small back bedroom, still trying to talk above the music. He forgot all about his offer of food until I mentioned a cup of coffee when he came back out to change the record.

"Oh yeah. And some good whole wheat monk's bread, with fresh butter." And, as an afterthought: "You don't want any of that cheese this time of morning, do you?"

For just a moment . . . a blank stare between us.

"Anyway, sit down here at my desk and I'll put on some Coltrane, the greatest sound in jazz saxophone right now. —To eat by!" he announced with a big grin.

It took only a few seconds to know that I wasn't quite ready for the Coltrane sound. "Uh uh, Tom, this stuff's too progressive for my untrained city ear."

And when he came back into the room carrying the coffee and toast, I let him know by my squinty frown that I wouldn't be able to digest my food to such "a cacophony of screeching noise!"

"Great jazz," he assured me. "You talk like Jacques and John Howard. . . . Okay though — you just take your time. Doctor's appointment not until nine. I'll finish dressing."

Tom's probably right, I told myself sitting there. He does know his jazz. After all, he was sort of a part-time pianist in Greenwich Village while a student . . . nevertheless . . . .

I listened for as long as I could, then stood up and lifted the arm off the phonograph, careful not to scratch his *OM* album, and sat back down at the desk.

Through the large window I could see the valley beyond the tunnel of trees stretching away on both sides. The knob hills far off were taking shape. "It's getting light. Can see through the fog now," I said over my shoulder as Tom came back into the room.

He was wearing this almost Groucho Marx disguise of beret and dark glasses. He stood there looking at me, smiling, with some kind of glowing pride.

"I don't want to be recognized by anyone in town. You know, there've been a few photographs in the paper and some magazines lately." —He was somewhat embarrassed by the exposure, this unsought and unwelcome kind of publicity.

But I could only laugh at the sight of him.

Another view from the hermitage porch, with meadow and distant knob hills draped in fog.

"You look more like Picasso. . . . —Either learn to paint damned fast, or take 'em off."

"That bad, eh?" he asked.

"Worse. . . .You look like Jean Genet," I laughed, whistling. —It won't work. Besides, nobody's going to notice you. . . . Merton, remember, not Mailer. It'll be night and crowded at the jazz joint anyway."

"Probably right. —But I'll take 'em along just in case," turning, through the kitchen, back to his small bedroom to get his jacket. "Gonna bring along your Blues manuscript to read as we ride in, okay?" Tom yelled around the corner.

"Yeah, sure. . . . Better get going. Take our time driving."

Tom back again, wearing his standard olive-drab cloth jacket, hands-in-pockets. Stopping to look down at my hiker boots, "Hey, you're gonna be doing some dancing to the jazz tonight, eh? Not in those. . . . Change into your pointy black Joe's Palm Room sliders later. Yeah."

Locking the door of the hermitage behind us, we got into the car and circled around through the grass and onto the dirt road, down through the swinging gate and right on 247 for a slow three-mile window-gaping tourist drive past Nelson County country landscape.

"Not much different, eh, from what you describe in your trip here, *Out of the South — Blues*". . . tapping the back of my manuscript against the dashboard. "Rain-washed unpainted falling-down wood shacks. Broke-window shutter-bang abandoned ghost rooms. Fire-black cinder rubble with lone chimney-stand, not even a bird perching . . . 's what we got along here now, for sure."

"Did you bring the camera," I asked, slowing the car at the junction of 31–E. "Oughta be a picture of that old fishing hole before it too disappears."

"Naw. We'd be forever stopping, never get to Louisville. . . . Like that old tin beer sign with rusty bullet holes nailed to the porchpost of the beer-joint there," Tom pointed as I turned right for another eight miles of winding road before we hit Bardstown.

"Car broke down in a midnight snowstorm here once," crossing the steel-girdered bridge over a creek, "'had to walk the last mile into town, not knowing a soul," I said, stopping at the light in front of the Cathedral before turning right on 62 a short block, then left again on 3rd Street, bypassing Bardstown Road business traffic, taking 1430 for a hilly two miles of clean suburbs till we hit Highway 245 for another thirteen-mile leg of blacktop heading for the 65 turnpike that would speed us on into Louisville — all in all, just an hour's drive if you want to make time.

But we were on the Bernheim Road now heading west and time was the white line of the pavement stretching away above the shine of our hood and feeding in fast under the left front wheel and out again behind us back Bardstown way. Nothing now for us but "eyes to the moving."

"Reach down, Tom, get some music on the radio — WLOU Louisville if it'll come in. We must have sound to our motion."

Tom smiling, bending to the dial, "And maybe a few cold beers a shortways up ahead to fuel our vision too, yes!"

"Be nice eh, to hear. . . . a harmonica whining, a guitar *baaa-whanging*, a drum *stomp-booming* out of the dimming distance—the lowdown voice of Chicago street-shouter Muddy Waters mouthing the blues on midmorn WLAC Nashville radio miles below to the South" (remembering almost verbatim the lines in my manuscript still unopened on the seat between us).

But Tom, still tuning the dial on the dashboard, caught it — and looking up with a big grin, grabbed the bundle of pages and started shaking them in front of my face with "Ah, your old hitchhike road-write when young . . . I know that sing!" —laughing. "And gonna give you some more of it, like I promised back at the hut," now flipping through the pages to find where I left off.

"Oh no, please — at least one beer first, before that!"

"Sorry. But you stuck it in the ear of the Editor of *Monks Pond* . . . and kind editor responds in kind. —Ah, here tis," holding the spread page high and reading right at me:

> And all the time the same music everywhere in the night throughout the South comes to me unheard—
> The yellow halfmoon glow of a radio in the window sill, playing the same moaning voice.
> Beneath scattered tin roofs, bedrooms filled with Texas hillblues Howlin' Wolf, a voice wavering on the air, crying

> > That's eeevil . . .
> > Evil's goin on

> Lightnin' Hopkins, a huge head thrust in the open doorway—

> > Gonna make pretty women
> > Jump 'n shout

> A sound out of the sideroads.
> In haylofts beneath P R I N C E   A L B E R T paint under the moon.
> Through all the sackcloth windows set back in the darkness.
> The music settling on the plowed fields that await the early morning feet of the workers with hanging heavy hands. The men with the hoes. —After the night . . . when moaning bluesmen Memphis Slim and Preacher Stevens are through with them.

Silence. —Then the faint sound of the tires whirring the pavement. Waiting for the light emptiness in my stomach to go.

Finally, "That's good. What you gave there. And what I want — that *feeling* of the music. . . . What I hope to get tonight. Jazz — the deep *living* in it," Tom said very softly, looking into the windshield. Then, "I think we could both use that beer now. . . . there, up ahead, on your left.

Back on the highway now and five more miles along, having given up on the radio, we sat silent, from time to time nodding our heads in the direction of something of interest the side of the road, until Tom raised his hand cupping the cold can of beer and pointed ahead to the right, "The distillery, JIM BEAM — laugh factory for Gethsemani's fruitcakes. . . . Go Big Jim."

"Photography there. We could take pictures of the workers entering in the morning, and then again leaving in the afternoon. See if a light meter detects any change in their eyes. . . . But you and your buddy Ed Rice, or was it Meatyard, have already shot the distilleries full of holes with your zoom lens," I said.

"Yeah, but those were in the name of art. Hang in galleries. Bring big prices. Money to go back to the monastery to give to the distillery to get more bourbon to make more fruitcakes to sell to you and Sally for money to buy me more film to take pictures of the distillery. . . . Quaker Oat box cycle of eternal return."

"Beercan talk. No more for you, Tom. —You're starting to make sense."

A sign: *APPROACHING* BERNHEIM FOREST next to a railroad crossing. I turn my head to see the rails running their shine alongside the road and, far behind us but gaining, see a dark line of boxcars bending the curve and the light of a diesel engine break through the brush now closeby and, crashing the crossing, howl its whistle wailing through the valley in a mournful wake-up warning of *Look Out!* the *Train L&N is bashing thru* right on past us into Bowling Green far ahead down the line.

"At least it looks like *they* know where they're going," Tom laughed, " — as for our way . . . no way . . . wu-wei."

"Not so . . . I know (at least I *knew*) where I'm going — at least then, seven or eight years ago," slowing down, pulling off the road onto the gravel shoulder and stopping the car.

"Right over there . . .," I began to say but Tom was *ssshhh*-ing me.

"Hold on a second now," tuning the radio dial again to clear the static, bring it in clear. "Listen," he said, leaning his ear to the speaker in the dashboard, turning up the volume.

> . . . in her right hand
> A silver dagger
> She says that I can't
> be your bride

"Joan Baez . . . that song. A couple years—"

"Wait . . . wait — listen," Tom said, holding his hand up,

> Go court another tender maiden
> And hope that she will be your wife
> For I've been warned and I've decided
> To sleep alone all of my life

the high trilling voice fading off into the *hhmmm*-ing distance.

Tom held the dial between his fingers a few seconds, then clicked the radio off and straightened up, sitting silent, staring through the windshield. Then — "Damn. . . . Can you believe it?. . . And right here, at just this moment," turning his head and nodding towards the entrance to Bernheim Forest across the road.

"Synchronicity!" I announced with raised palms. "Happens all the time."

But Tom not taken by the energy and enthusiasm in my voice. The 'coincidence' may be a little too much for him just now.

"Yeah, I know — This place . . . brings some of that all back . . . the thing with 'M'."

"Over there, back that road, down near the lake . . . a picnic," Tom mumbled slowly, more to himself than to me.

"Why I pulled over and stopped," I said. "Was going to tell you about my first date with Sally . . . a picnic! — and right down beside that same lake," looking over to Tom. "Old Bernheim Forest—whew! . . . some kind of sacred space, eh?"

"Do you think we could just drive back over through there for a while? We've got plenty of time . . . no hurry, really," Tom almost whispering.

"Naw, don't think so. Place not even open yet," I told him, my voice flat — disappointed too.

Right — probably for the best anyway. . . . That's all over. Part of the past now. —Just as well," Tom's voice lifting.

"Yeah, but I gotta tell you about Sally and myself, how it was, how it turned out, and what it really meant to me . . . for the rest of my Life!"

Tom was grinning now, feeling better. "Okay. Hear up, every-body! . . . The story now, very brief, of history's greatest love!"

"Naw, naw — nothing like that. Just that I was twenty-five years old at the time and trying to make up my mind whether to become a monk, or run off to Paris to live as a suffering poet — or stay right home here in Kentucky and marry the most beautiful girl I had ever met! . . . Some choice, eh? —Well, not as easy as it might first appear. After all, as a Catholic I was told over and over again all the way through grammar and high school the hierarchy of the spiritual life . . . which went something like this: highest vocation: the cloistered contemplative (you know, a monk, eh Tom); next highest: the ordinary priest (for the boys only, of course); still high: the brother or nun (time to include the girls); lower: the single layperson who devotes entire life to the Church; lowest: shame oh shame; all the rest who decide to love another human being and get married. . . . How's that for maintaining the ol self-esteem, eh? Makes a guy like me, incurably horny! . . . feel like a real scumbag in the eyes of the Lord. Well if you can't do anything else, then get married, sayeth the Church."

"Get to the horny part!" Tom yelled, laughing (mimicking his favorite line from a Lenny Bruce routine).

"Okay, I will — they, Father "H," wouldn't admit me as a monk at Gethsemani, and I tried several times, because they said I was too horny, . . . no, not in those exact words, but others telling me the same . . . and to be honest, they were right. —Hell, in a matter of a few days behind those walls, I would have been drawing naked ladies in the dirt with a stick.

"Well, to get back to my picnic with beautiful Sally over there beside Lake of the Bernheim — as I said, almost twenty-six years old, and Tom . . . she is only a petal-fresh young flower just past her eighteenth birthday!"

"Yes, Yes. You must continue," Tom said seriously, hunched over as if he were scribbling notes on an imaginary pad.

"We're sitting on a blanket spread beneath a shade tree next to the rippling sun-speckled water, she in an of off-the-shoulder pink cotton summer dress with pale cheeks now flushed below her brilliantly shining red hair tumbling long down her back too soft-looking even for my breath to touch . . . and me lying back leisurely propped on one elbow sipping wine with one hand and eating grapes with the other, looking at the light flashing through the leaves lifting her face cupped in the U of her palms framing her eyes sparkling bright at mine."

"I see . . . but was the setting *romantic*?" Tom inquired objectively.

"Yes, yes, I think you've caught it. . . that's the word, exactly. —From that moment I knew I never had a chance! No more the thoughts of monkery. Down on the rocks of time with poesy. Now and forevermore a life as lover!"

"And let the horny rot in Hell!" Tom slammed his fist down *bam* on the dashboard. "—Period. End of story. End of celibacy. Beginning of Life for Ron Seitz . . . who now will pull his car back onto the road and continue his journey to Louisville."

Which I did.

A fast half-hour drive, arriving in town on time for the first doctor's appointment, and the second. Then over to the lawyer's office. On to the Merton Center at the College for an intense hour's work and finished just in time to make it downtown for lunch.

Cunningham's was one of Tom's favorite eating places in Louisville. Located at 5th and Breckinridge Streets in the inner city, the old restaurant did have a certain unique atmosphere, if not the highest sanitation rating. There were private wooden booths in the far rear room where Tom liked to meet his friends (Jim Wygal, "M," Father John) to talk and laugh and eat huge deep-fried fish sandwiches, the specialty, with steak fries and large round steins of draft beer.

We arrived a little after noon but, much to Tom's disappointment, all the booths were occupied. The waiter had to push a couple of tables together up front by the door to accommodate about five other people waiting for us. And although these were some of Tom's closest friends, he felt uncomfortable sitting there out in public with so many people passing through the door next to him.

After everyone was settled I found myself seated next to Tom, on the right, and J. Laughlin sat next to him on the left, almost opposite me. This proved to be an awkward position for Tom because he and J had not seen each other for some time and wanted to catch up on some serious business about writing and publishing, and I (being a young unwashed upstart in the world of letters) was somewhat nervous but more curious about this, to me, 'famous' publisher of New Directions books (undoubtedly the most influential house of international major poets in this century). As they talked, I leaned to listen, so as not to miss any important give-and-take information. (An imposition upon their privacy, and unforgiveably rude behavior, I know I know, but . . . .)

I had just bitten into my sandwich when I caught J's voice saying something to the effect that "Right, *Lolita* was mine to publish but I let it get away . . . someone said it was too controversial, obscene if you really want to know" — and I burst across Tom, my mouth full of fish, saying something about Nabokov's book being a masterpiece and how could J, a responsible publisher, allow someone else to influence his critical judgement on something as important as that. Tom was obviously embarrassed, leaning back in his chair to avoid my sputtering face, telling me I had gotten it all wrong and hadn't heard the entire story (something about not wanting to hurt the feeling of J's aunt being the real reason). Or maybe that was the case a few minutes later when I, uninvited, offered my views on J not publishing Henry Miller's two *Tropics* but most of his other books, again the word obscene being an issue. —The entire scene turning into a disaster because I so wanted "to belong" to this special group of gifted people (my unbounded love of poetry, theirs too, the real reason), the lunch ending prematurely with only one stein of beer and J, whom I had tried to touch, seemingly oblivious to my presence.

So, off again with Tom to visit a few homes, make a brief pass through the University library, and back to the O'Callaghan home for a short rest before a shower and shave, ready for dinner at a 'finer' restaurant in the business district near the river before meeting again at our final distination — Eddie's Place, at 118 Washington Street.

Tom had broken away from the others at the "fine folded-napkin whitecoat waiter-bowing swank maître d' finger-snap ushered soup-chapel" (as he bouncingly described it). . . . and arrived early to stand with Sally and myself in the narrow cobblestone street out front of the club — an old abandoned brick warehouse with red neon *J A Z Z* blinking us off and on in the wrapping darkness. We would wait for the others to arrive.

"Melville must have been the exterior decorator for this place," Tom said. "Time, I think, to put this thing on," blowing his breath white on the air as he pulled the beret out of his coat pocket (a sort of heavy rain poncho loaned him by someone no doubt surreally bent) — stretching the cap down low, almost touching his ears, to cover his moisting bald head.

The damp dark air and cold mist fogging off the river had Sally wrapped around my arm, pressing close to keep from shivering.

"Picasso or Jean Genet would be a welcome sight now, Tom," I said as his face blinked on red. Then out again gone black as I added: "Better chance though it be ol Jack-a-Rippin round the corner. . . . Let's get the hell on inside."

Hurrying through the door, we found a large empty table just inside, far to the rear and back from the bandstand.

A few minutes later, the rest of the crowd arrived, got settled. With everyone finally seated now, Tom put his dark glasses on, glancing across the table at Sally, baring his teeth with a big smile.

Just as the last drink was ordered all around, a crack of light opened and closed across the table, a waft of cold air touched my back, and there was J just inside the door now standing directly behind me. I turned and looked up to see him tall, loose, both hands in a well-worn slouch raincoat held open, then heard Sally's whisper of "handsome, like Gary Cooper." He slowly pulled a chair up and sat down a few feet behind and between us. As Tom's fellow poet, publisher, and close friend these many years, he was just content, fondly amused to be in his company and, leaning back with hands clasped in his lap, moved his eyes over the long dark room, a nod hello to someone and another, saying little if anything.

But the fact that J. Laughlin sat only a few feet away made me anxious. Here, again, the man who had studied with Ezra Pound, lived with Gertrude Stein, known William Carlos Williams and Eliot and everybody else who was somebody in the far-off world of modern letters in this century . . . and who I had just met for the first time that day at lunch, making a complete fool of myself . . . this intimidated me. To the point that, once more, in my youth and ignorance and inexperience, I became angry. I was threatened by his calmness, his self-composure, his apparent confidence in who he was.

"Laconically sardonic," I muttered to myself and anyone else who might hear.

But this was all of my own making. He was kind and softspoken. Yet when he leaned forward and quietly asked Sally, "And are you a poet, too?". . . . I took it as a cynical putdown of my being considered that by Tom (and that just a polite compliment as a friend), but himself not at all impressed by what work of mine he had seen through Tom. This the reason I had been frantically scribbling words of outrage and protest in my notebook on my knee in the dark under the table. —All of this self-conscious anxious anger closing me until. . . .

The first notes of the quartet sounded sharply on the air, coming out of the light dimmed blue on the bandstand, riding the darkness above all the heads in front of us . . . and the barrier between J and myself crumbled. The music joined us. And with Sally and the others, we too watched as Tom sat bolt upright in his chair, fully attentive and receptive to what these four musicians were about to do in that circle of blue, an island of light afloat now on the sound flowing towards us.

"They're going to start talking to each other now. Listen," Tom whispered, leaning across the table.

But Tom could stand being that far removed from the music only so long. *Sssshhhh*-ing, he quietly left the table to move down closer. I watched him snaking his way through the crowd until he was at the edge of the bandstand, squatting low and close (so as not to distract but to see and be better with the music).

Standing now, I watched the back of Tom's head move up and down with the bassman's fingers — his eyes become worn calloused skin running *thump thump tha thump* the taut thick strings, his head bobbing to the time-pause thumb-pluck of sound the same as the caught-breath blank-space phrasing of silence on the page in poetry.

Now the bassman bent further to coddle his left arm tight to the long lean neck of wood and press his right thigh warm to the wide-shine double bellow and hump note-by-note his *say* to the waiting hands poised above the piano keys until they overlap link the sound to come *tink tink dum tink* from the thin spread fingers gliding high then dropping delicate a push-lift of new pitch *clink clink* running his roll of rhythm notes to slide the stick that *knacks* a rim-shot running a jolt back the drummer's arm to message the hands to flutter the tips of wood on the sprung skin *drrey drump* snare-call to foot-felt *boom hh boom* hollow bounce off gold-click alto-valves breathing the reed *wwhhaau whuu* and off on *fleep ba wheep* floops bleeps and whips of weeps finally fusing the four in chorus *rraaagghh eh rruuugh remmpf!* cut, out, off, close . . . silence, now bows.

The set had run almost fifteen minutes. Sally and I stood the entire time, to watch Tom follow the 'conversation' moving from one player to the next to another, back and forth, one to one, all to one, one to all.

Tom had been completely swept away, borne off with the music — jazz, the pure sound of it. He crouched with eyes and face raised to the sight of it. . . . nodding his head *yes yes* — a shoulder-hunched urging on of the bassman to new highs with "Give it! Give . . . Here! Here! . . . now Take it!" — pumping notes one to one, artist to artist — the sweet sweat eye-bond holding them both on that one wave riding out and over . . . gone with it.

Then Tom standing to applaud-praise the bald black bass player with open palms of "Yeah! Yeah! . . . Alright, that's it!" . . . *Thanks.*

The knowing nodding return-touch of the musician enough to acknowledge the 'bond'. . . What everyone in the place could see, but didn't — because the others at our table, with the exception of J, had gone back to their toasts and talk (another kind of conversation) once the first few notes of the set had sounded.

And coming back to the table, eyes wide, serious, Tom said, "Now that's praying. . . . That's some kind of prayer! . . . the new liturgy. —Really, I'm not kidding. Closer than most of us'll ever get to it."

Sally and I nodded, smiling.

"We'll come back again, eh?" Tom leaned across the table, almost whispering. "Some of us, thanks to Yardbird, still enjoy Church."

"You bet," I mumbled, not even looking up but, now feeling a touch of sadness, just stared into the orange flicker of flame of the candle lighting the glass bowl in the center of the table. My eyes on the small *flep* of fire darkening everything else out and away as my lips pursed "True."

———◆———

"True," I said, staring at the last short flames flaring off the crumbled glowing logs on the floor of the fireplace. Sitting hunched in the rocker, the hermitage gone cold again, thinking:

I understood then. . . . I understand now. Even moreso.

Because Tom was so alive with enthusiam about so many things (seemingly unlimited)—as a dynamic vital porous poet should be. It was contagious, this creative spirit. And manytimes (all-at-once) I too would be talking excitedly about the 'possibilities' of so many things.

And this innocent attribute of acute sensitivity and receptivity (really 'vulnerability') is probably what some detractors of Tom describe as his 'naivete'.

Ha! . . . . what a wit-loss to be accused of that.
Tom just had an open-ended unprejudiced accommodation to all
    manner and expression of beauty.
So — not indiscriminate. Just a refusal to be smugly judgemental.
Tom Merton — a true Buddha. . . . in the sense of being compassion-
    ately available to and touching All!

"All so long ago," I say aloud as I lift the blanket off of my knees
and push myself up out of the rocker. —But now, the memory of
some of what made me angry that day, seems funny . . . especially
my fumbling first meetings with J, and my angry counterattack
scribbled in the notebook under the table while at the jazz joint —
a disjointed anti-poem transcribed verbatim from secret scrawl for
all world to see — sent along to Tom on long teletype sheet which
doubled him up in bursts of laughter every few lines as he read

Jottings for Poem in Memory of Night-Jazz with J. Laughlin

who was that sat beside me in silence deaf to jazz?
some lean handsome giant Gary Cooper western hero kind
    in long wrinkle overcoat droopy hobo hat
World Letters mystery figure stepped from Sylvia Beach
    photo hanging Paris 20s bookshop wall
much too suave & "been there" for me anxious unknowing young—

leaning chiselled jaw to jazzy darkness above table
casually walking thru Pound's insanity Canto book in hand
touching Williams Miller Corso Merton work with finger first

O that you had not been there the cause
pissing my pants in nervous yearning at what I had NOT done—
epic poems composed in eyes only!
if you had only read THOSE then maybe once looked at me
instead of lofty glance past this shaking face in the darkness

must I say Damn You! Dear J—
come to that in my weary fear & frustration among vision heroes
as you lope the pavement of literary legend
while I shudder my dreaming years cracked down the middle
    by rejection

O I don't think you want my beauty, ND—
would not have the taste for it to ski the Alps chop wood
    in Conneticut swim Mediterranean waters
& not having seen myself print paper bound in book maybe never
New York the city still scares

that's my sad story no New Direction
& yr tears'll not drop in my palms because
it could have been otherwise if LITERATURE were more loving—
but that's another poem
unpublished

to the end, shouting, "Send it to him! . . . or I'll publish it in *Monks Pond*" — but neither would do as Tom dutifully fueled the fire with it.

A few logs dropped on the glowing ashes and flaming again. Now to the kitchen and boil the water for my tea, cut a wedge of that aged monk's cheese with the good strong smell, two slices of the fresh whole wheat bread from the monastery bakery this morning — ah thinking of that thick sandwich late lunch while the tea bag soaks the water dark and tart to the tongue.

I've got a few minutes to step into the tiny chapel behind me and drop my knee to leather pad and lean elbows across the slanted wood and clasp hands in a finger-fold prayer of raising my eyes to the small cross on the wall behind the square cloth-draped altar, a metal tabernacle to the left and three ikons surrounding the cross catching the light through the front window. I bow my head to the complete silence, kneel a few moments, then rise and light the single candle at the rear corner of the altar.

Chapel in Merton's hermitage.

Standing in front of the stove eating my sandwich and sipping my hot tea, I lean to the back wall and look at the small black-on-black painting, a cross, by Tom's friend, Ad Reinhardt. I have to smile at the holy indifference of the monks who have cooked various foods on these gas burners and unaware in their *Zen Eat Ceremonies* have splattered grease onto the work of one of the most renowned modernist painters in America. Oh well, a 'Tao Baptism of Art'. . . . a healthy way to interpret the Providence in posterity.

Now the total homage in the sacrament of washing and rinsing the tea cup and replacing it on the hook, then I can enter the back bedroom and lie down a few minutes on the checked quilt covering Tom's small cot in the corner against the rear wall. A comfortable bed because gratuitous and a blessed privilege to rest here where Tom had.

I cross my hands upon my chest, close my eyes, and lie completely still. Stop the interior monologue and image-conjuring. Empty. Receptive. Waiting for *poverty*.

Out . . . five, ten minutes at most . . . now back. Totally refreshed.

And still lying here, the memory of the dream begins rising to the surface. I sit, reach over and pick up my notebook and pen

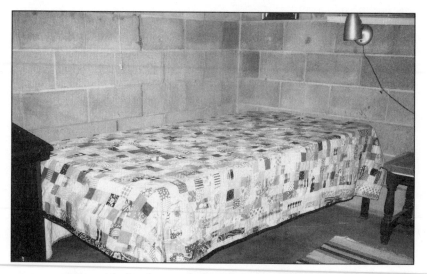

Merton's bed in the sparely furnished room of his hermitage.

from the small table at the head of the bed and, as quickly as possible, begin writing the Dream already fading to:

> the monastery, the Abbey of Gethsemani. There are five of us there: myself, Tom Merton, Dan Walsh, Father John Loftus, and John Howard Griffin.
> We are gathered outside, down and away in front of Tom's hermitage, sort of separated, spread out about ten yards apart, in not quite a circle, and standing up to our waists in tall blowing grass (going golden-brown, like wheat), our faces slightly tilted up and lit by the sun.
> All of us are smiling, laughing easily, relaxed, again at peace, sort of talking and yelling back and forth to each other, nothing of 'real consequence or import' really being said, just an expression of the joy of being! . . . childlike, innocent, the love of each other 'connecting' us in our small community.
> Again, it is 'understood' and 'accepted' that Tom and Father John and Dan and John Howard had died, are 'dead to the world' . . . I am aware of this, as well as the fact that I am 'different' — I am alive.
> A strong concrete visual image (apparently significant): all five of us are standing out in this field of tall grass and the sun is cutting a line across the land, with Tom and Father John and Dan standing in the shade, myself in the sun, and John Howard with one foot in each.
> Although the most recent to die, John Howard's 'condition' or 'state' is not really determined. He is with us in the group and accepted as an essential member of it, but is not like them, the dead, or like myself, obviously still among the living. And, strangely, I am aware of his not 'belonging to either of these categories' but am not concerned about it — in fact, utterly indifferent about his 'existence-status' . . . because we are all united in the *one* of joy and love.

And now, sitting on the edge of the bed and looking down at the words scrawled across the pages of my notebook, I realize that in all of these dreams about my closest friends, without exception, there is a great joyous climate of laughter, 'having a good time', calm, relaxed . . . in a word, *peace!*

I think of the dream and begin to read what I've written and, putting the notebook down on the bed, tell myself that I have always considered (in fact, *known*) that my life would include these four 'chosen' persons to be God's loving instrument (whatever the divine reason), for my *conversion*: Thomas Merton, Dan Walsh, John Loftus, and John Howard Griffin. And myself, in all humility (and gratitude), was 'grouped' with these people to form this five-pointed star — that I, for whatever 'crooked purpose', was necessary for the group unit. . . . This doesn't necessarily mean (and I feel sure it to be the case) that the others involved (all four of them) were aware of this connection, or looked upon me as one of those very few intimate friends we have in our 'passing-thru'. —In fact, I feel quite confident that each of us (as a member) branched off from his person-point to form another 'cluster', and on to infinity, possibly to include and gather everyone who has ever lived. . . . So, what my star had in common with Dan's and Father John's and John Howard's is that we were all members each to each. And what just might be so absolutely essential about the dream is that we all four had shared a mutual love relationship with Tom Merton, which draws the bond even tighter and holds me even now, the very moment, to this living dream experience!

Up from the cot now I stand looking out the small bedroom window to the low stone wall behind the hermitage, creekrock stacked years ago by monks for some special purpose long abandoned — where Tom and I sat one afternoon, much like this one, the winter before he left and (for a "very special purpose") talked long and long.

Walking through the kitchen I go into the chapel, blow out the candle still flickering, then turn back to the front room to put on my jacket and open the door onto the porch.

A wave of cold air hits my chest as I fumble with the buttons of my jacket before stepping onto the smooth concrete.

I stand a moment taking deep breaths of the winter air, check my side pocket for notebook and pen, then clomp the hard rubber soles of my hiker boots three steps across the porch and hop down onto the grass to walk alongside and behind the hermitage until I come to the wall, just a short distance away.

I place my bare palm atop the flat ridged stone and let the rough cold feel spread through my fingers — the *touch* to run my body and bring back first the *memory of place*.

There.

Now the 'rest of it' coming (Tom and I together talking) as I turn and sit on the wall—

Stone wall at which author and Merton frequently held their long give-and-take discussions.

We were sitting the wall, side by side, Tom shaking his head as he talked about the 'controversial' (to some, scandalous) "affair with the nurse."

All of that was over now, had been for some time. But Tom, knowing that the 'situation' had hurt so many people — especially his own family, the community of monks — and some of his very close friends, Dan Walsh in particular. . . .

"Who really don't understand in the slightest what it was all about," Tom said in a burst of frozen breath clouding his face.

And even though he had written "honestly and completely" about the entire matter in his journals and in many poems — he said that he needed to "get it out, once and for all. . . voice it for myself if no one else."

So here he was again, hopefully "one last time . . . . clearing the air" with someone "who just might have an inkling of who he was (and "M" too)" — what "really happened in all this."

Tom's words then coming crisp and clear on the cold air. A staccato rhythm to his speech because obviously in a hurry, anxious to have it over and done with.

The sound of his voice so close made me shift my buttocks on the stone ledge and lean back, looking up through the branches of the tree directly behind us. —Why me? I asked myself. . . . Because of all of that stuff I'd told him over the years about my conflict between loving a woman and embracing a monastic vocation (or following an 'artistic calling' for that matter) — a so-called 'problem' that he could relate to. . . . Well, from what Tom told me of his romantic experiences before entering the monastery, I was, by comparison, a "novice in matters of love" (and a good chance his struggle tougher than mine).

Tom had pushed himself off the wall and now walked back and forth in front of me, rubbing his hands and *wwhhhooo*-ing his frozen breath as he talked. To suddenly stop and, shuffling his boots in the deep leaves, turn and wait for me to lower my eyes to his. —And what did I think about all this?

Sticking my hands in my jacket pockets and hunching forward to the cold, I could only mutter a few words to the effect that what had happened was "all too-human" and that he was really a better man for it.

That not enough for Tom. Specifics. He wanted *specifics*!

Never mind that I had told him more than once before, and now did again — that what had happened between him and "M" was understandable, and for a number of reasons. . . . First, being a 'healthy' male, fifty years old (a 'crisis' time for many men), and being celibate for some twenty-five years, he had been in a quite vulnerable situation to say the least: a hospital patient being nursed by a beautiful young woman for an extended time. And to compound the matter even more, he was under the influence of heavy pain medication (quite often an effective aphrodisiac). That coupled with his close and direct contact in a patient-nurse relationship (hands-on care) was a volatile mix.

"Sounds like a drink," Tom said with a quick laugh. And, as before when I would mention such notions, Tom dismissed all this with a wave of the hand and, "Quack diagnosis."

I sat there and looked at Tom standing only five feet away, his back to me now, and knew that he wanted something else, something more. But I could only offer what I had earlier — a flat out expression of my thoughts about his "experience" with "M": That in his heart of hearts he never really intended to leave his monastic life and run off, marry, and live with this woman (or any woman for that matter). Not that he wasn't tempted and truly enjoyed 'toying with the temptation' (and this not a frivolous consideration). It wasn't that he had been 'using' this woman to satisfy a curiosity or to test himself in any way. Nothing even approaching that.

I reminded Tom of what, to me, seemed so obvious: that nothing less than the highest spiritual state (for him, the solitary contemplative) could ever satisfy his insatiable longing for sanctity. — For Tom Merton it was all or nothing, now or never . . . and nothing or no-body would or could steer him away or astray from his lifelong pilgrimage.

Tom had turned back around when he no longer heard my voice. He walked a few steps through the leaves and stopped to lean against a tree. He stood with both hands in his pockets, looking at me.

He did not say anything for a long time. And it wasn't that he disagreed with me now (or then, earlier, when we talked about this "nurse issue" while it was still happening) — it was just that he seemed to want to delay the decision, wanted to deny that the two choices were mutually exclusive for him and his monastic vocation.

He looked at me with a pained expression, shaking his head in an apparent gesture of resistance, a belated refusal to admit that he would have to relinquish one "love" for the other.

There was a deep sad hurt in his eyes as he stood there silently, looking the dilemma straight on. It was as heart-wrenching a struggle as I've ever witnessed. But he knew, and I knew, that it had to be suffered, gone through, and put behind him — then when it was alive . . . and now, again, to be able to live with it.

Then slapping his palms together in a loud *plaapp*! and, "That's the sound of two hands clapping," Tom was walking towards me.

He scooted onto the wall a few feet away and, leaning forward with his hands on his knees, said: "It's something that eats at the heart. Literally. . . . They followed us here, Ron. Never left us. . . . We've been carrying her, them, with us all this time — just as the young monk in the Zen story did, long after the old Master had put the woman down after carrying her across the stream.

"We just sit here on this wall, waiting for *them* to leave us." Turning to me, "Them". . . who are *us*, really. Eh, Ron?"

Tom's last words, "Them! . . . who are *us*, really," — rang loud in my ears and stayed there. That's it! I told myself . . . that's why he's telling *me* all this. —My statement!

Just the week before I had written him a letter that included a somewhat 'radical pronouncement' offered in one of my lectures on feminist theology (which also included a transcript of Sally's tape of the talk), a somewhat playful piece that turned out more serious than I intended—

Dear Tom,

A few hours freedom tonight to write you a light letter concerning a recent spiritual sojourn of mine into the hazardous terrain of Tongued-Cheek Theology.

Last week I guest-lectured at the college in a course entitled "Feminine Perspectives in Contemporary Theology." (I know, I know – why trade in your used Purgatory for a new Hell?)

The subject of the discussion (should there be one) was tentatively, "What is a nice young woman like you doing in a Church like this?". . . or words to that effect.

And in that audience of rapt listeners to a prophet of silly pronouncements sat the Congress of Sorrows – those keepers of ten thousand items of household (the mouthwash, toilet-paper, clean sheets, lightbulbs, where's-a-pencil?) who had stepped from the stifling air of domesticity into the (seemingly) liberating air of radical freedom-of-conscience brewed from the smoldering cauldron of NEW THEOLOGY. These women (already purged by pangs of terminal patriarchy) would taste the void of doubt and disbelief, a flirtatious jaunt onto the fringe of righteous rebellion, and (the Pope permit) rub lobes with the intoxication of low-key heresy.

I would address their appetite for 'religious titillation'.
Me, a loose-sprung fallen poet who had ranted his melancholy
malcontent in this declining decade of social-civil active
unrest. And now near spent of that cause, I would turn my
eyes and heated heart to their 'ultimate concerns' of
spirituality—

LET US NOW DISCUSS, WITH UTMOST SERIOUSNESS, THE
QUESTION OF GOD AND (more particularly) HIS ONLY
BEGOTTEN SON, JESUS CHRIST.

And there I was, the bearded 'professor', with what ulterior
motive of self-aggrandizement and esthetic vanity, to throw them
a bone of contention, some cerebral morsel to whet what crave for
controversy to carry back to numb dumb insensitive unlistening
male-mates, to badger them with their only new weapon in a
rapidly disappearing arsenal of defense offensives to maintain
their autonomy and human dignity involuntarily abdicated long
ago with the barbarous economic barter of sex for security — their
staunch stance on a truly serious matter, the matter of Faith, the
Catholic Church, and Christianity itself!

Such was my insidiously seductive challenge. And I would set
forth a premise of possibility (hastily considered and not thought
through) — not so much to convince, persuade, or convert to a
position (because I myself could and would deflate it later under
close scrutiny), but just to prick their conscience, provoke self-
examination, elicit thought, and sow the strengthening seeds of
speculative skepticism absolutely necessary to an authentic Rite
of Conversion . . . that is, to entertain the most outrageous,
farflung, heretical fringes of the traditional orthodox body of
Christian belief.

And so be it: that night (forgive me, Lord, for this self-indulgent
mitered pose of enlightened proselytizing) I began by printing in

large writ, with a piece of chalk on the newly-wiped clean blackboard, these words, this

STATEMENT

I AM A MAN, AND MY LIFE IS TO LOVE A WOMAN

*DO THAT WHOLLY, AND EVERYTHING ELSE IS INCLUDED
ANYTHING OTHER THAN THAT IS A SUBSTITUTE FOR IT*

*NOTHING ELSE NEED BE SAID ABOUT WHO OR WHAT I AM
AND WHY*

*IF GOD BECAME MAN, HE LOVED A WOMAN
WHO WAS ALSO GOD*

Ah, Tom, as regards the above lecture: "in the beginning is my end; in the end is my beginning"—
I won't tell you the response of those women to this Statement.
What would be yours in their place (or even your own)?
Might be interesting, in light of your One-ing as MONK-LOVER.

Enough said. Hope you take this in the Free Spirit say.

Peace,

Ron S

"Getting too cold out there," Tom said as he closed the door of the hermitage behind him. "Feel all stiff from sitting too long, not moving."He was bending one leg at the knee and swinging the other.

"I'll get the fire going," I said. My hands were red and hurt as I picked up a log beside the fireplace. "Plenty of wood right here. Won't have to go back out to get any."

"Sounds good," Tom grinned as he wrapped his arms across his chest. "Hug myself warm."

"Maybe the host could brew us up some hot tea. Get all cozy, like we're hermits or something."

"Okay, tea. But no monks cheese. Wouldn't be able to talk, or think."

I was bent over the fireplace trying to light the logs when Tom turned back from going to the kitchen. He was standing beside me with a piece of typed paper in his hand.

"Your letter the other day was more than casual conversation about all this . . . the statement part, eh."

I was right — that *was* the 'nerve' of our meeting and talking out there on the wall . . . the 'woman thing' and all.

"We'll look at it, talk a bit, answer a few questions maybe . . . but won't be as simple as we'd probably like."

With the fire blazing now and the room more than warm, Tom stood with the crook of his elbow on the mantel, holding the small jagged piece of paper in his other hand. "A few lines from your statement," motioning with his arm to "Sit in the rocker here. It's okay, I can stand."

And so I sat there, my shoes off, and felt my thick hunting socks warming as Tom turned away to start walking slowly around the room, pacing behind me before I heard him stop near his desk by the window.

"First of all I want you to know that I don't totally agree with what you have to say in this statement here — I couldn't, you know. . . . Easy to understand why, eh?" Laughing . . . "But that's not the point."

He walked over to the right of me and stopped, looking at the piece of paper and then into my eyes."There are some very good points here, and what I'd like to do is comment where I think there is something positive and possibly on target — sort as if I were you and explaining or defending this to others, a lecture or whatever."

He was silent a few moments again, then began—

"First of all, the response to the content, the intent of this piece should be stimulating. It is a positive statement in that it touches the nerve of the psychological, as well as some of the religious intimations about such basic issues as sex, celibacy, monasticism — in fact, almost the entire ball of wax, eh, of just what it means to be human."

That was the beginning. And continuing to walk back and forth in front of the fire, then across the room behind me, stopping from time to time at his desk, Tom went on to tell me (or himself, or everyone, or no one) that there are important implications in all of this concerning the fact, the truth, the full reality of the

Incarnation, of God becoming Man — that is, an actual man on all accounts. And the crux of the issue here was that Christ had to be a 'fully-realized', *healthy* (in the fullest sense of that word) human — not an exceptional 'purist-ideal' of a person, more angel or spirit than flesh.

And here Tom went to the heart of the matter about Christianity (as he put it), its 'living-revelation experience' in the everyday lives of people. He put special emphasis and significance regarding youth in this matter, because "today they are the ones who demand the 'real', the authentic, the moment-by-moment concrete *touch* of the Divine in their lives." Many of these people, he went on, see the man-woman, love-sex, mating-children relationship as the "elemental defining cell that names us human."

Tom stood a moment facing the bookcase, his back to me, apparently trying to gather his thoughts. Then turning, said, "From the natural I-Thou, me-other relation that defines us as social animals — with the Divine capacity, the human promise of being lover — we are truly redeemed as Sons of God. . . . Resurrection is in the fulfillment and the realization of this seed-potential creation gift — *the letting go to become Who you have always been!* . . . I can't say this enough."

Pausing — "Of course, this is the great calling, the grand challenge of the courage-faith-hope freedom of Being! that is absolutely necessary to a spiritual life . . . to the so-called 'salvation heaven trip' or what-have-you that the young speak of."

Tom walked right up to the edge of the rocker, stopped, and looking straight down at the piece of paper in his hand, said, "Let me read the first line of the statement. —It says, *I am a man, and my life is to love a woman.*

"Now that defines man as wholly dependent upon an *other* for the totality of his nature. And the human animal, being who and what he is biologically, psychologically, and the rest . . . *ones* with this other by sexual complimentariness (if there be such a word)," he said, laughing again. "Or rather polymorphous sexuality — the current psycho-political term now bandied about. Ol' Marcuse and his gang, eh?". . . Tom lightening up some now, beginning to enjoy his little 'lecture game' with me. He went on, saying (more or less) that to do all this humanly (that is, in love) involves the primary social unit, the family . . . as well as, most often, the usual procreative result, children, the lifeline of the species.

"And from this seed springs all society, with its culture, religions, art, politics, the whole grabbag that makes up human history. . . . So, that is why the basic, essential premise of this statement is in the very first line.

"And why the two line second stanza—

Do that wholly, and everything else is included
Anything other than that is a substitute for it

says just that: do that wholly and the rest of it — morals, ethics, law, etc. — follows or is included. . . . And the second line about anything other is a substitute means just that: all social, economic, religious, scientific, technological utopian ideas, ideals, and theories about how to solve man's dilemma (that is, his creative condition of being man and not God or angel) are so many good-intentioned (most often, to be sure) attempts to rectify a situation that was not met or satisfied in that first experience of awareness and consciousness of just what it means to be human.

"This is what anthropology, sociology, psychology, religion, art, and the rest are trying to tell us. No abstract, ideological, synthetic solution will satisfy the demand, the holy challenge, free and tragic gift of life," Tom pausing a moment here to see if I understood. . . . "Yes, *tragic* in the classic sense of the awareness and acceptance of man's limitations, his defining nature, and all that it implies to be fully alive!" —His words an obvious parody of my lecturing.

Tom appeared now to be a little agitated, seeming to suspect that I was becoming impatient with his lengthening explanation of this apparently simple statement of mine, but it was obvious that he was intent to see it through to the end — possibly more for his own benefit than mine. He spoke almost non-stop, extemporaneously, as if there were an inexhaustible reservoir of knowledge flowing from him without effort. It was as if he were driven now to forever exorcize this spiritual but fully human love-experience become life-crisis for him. And, ironically, even absurdly so — by using those few, by all accounts, insignificant words of mine . . . a "statement" that I could put some stock in (and possibly even live by), but which Tom could not accept or assimilate into his wisdom-vision as a Catholic priest, at least not as read or understood literally.

"Which brings us to the two line third stanza," Tom continued. "A simpler one, understood best through the previous lines: the identity crisis, man's search for meaning (a rationale for existence), his overriding anxiety about alienation, his encounter with the absurd — all these swallowed up in the love-life, the other-living.

"The question, Who or What Am I? . . . and Why? —there is no answer, what would be given us as the rational security and satisfaction of 'knowledge'—

Nothing else need be said about who or what I am or why

Obviously. —A person's presence is only to be realized! . . . As another once said, and better: Life is not a problem to be solved, but a mystery to be experienced. —And this, only in love!"

At long last (for him anyway), Tom had come to the final two line stanza—

If God became man, he loved a woman
who was also God

—twelve 'simple' but (for that) weighty words. Such words that undoubtedly would cause the most consternation among traditional orthodox theological and religious notions, understandings, interpretations, appreciations of the mystery and miracle of the Incarnation.

"Just who was Jesus? What kind of a person was he?" Tom asked in a softer voice as he turned, took a few steps, and propped his elbow on the stone mantel above the fireplace again.

"If I read the temper and consciousness of our time accurately (closing in on the year 2000) — there will be less and less interest in, or concern with, locating Jesus historically because the question of placing him in a patriarchal culture and time has led to a feminine backlash of sorts, whereby he is shifted to a matriarchal situation or place, and we — men and women, both human — can accept neither. . . . And there is a possible flirt with *heresy*, if such a creature still be around."

Tom began rubbing the palm of his hand across the top of his forehead and, "So these last two lines, for sure controversial, radically so, to many, are no concession either to men or to women . . . a very small crumb of pacification for anybody, eh?" pausing and holding his hand against the back of his neck. —"It is just a simple statement to the effect that if indeed Christ did appear on Earth in History (as reported, eh!), then what is said here would naturally follow if, in truth, he were the whole healthy human that 'this Christ' would have to be. . . . Anything 'less' would hardly be acceptable, especially among the young, at this particular moment in Western culture."

Dropping his arm from the mantel and looking away from the fire, Tom said (almost as an afterthought), "True, belief might hang in there like a pop poster on a sacristy wall . . ." — then turning back around, his voice more emphatic, "but, if not a living Christ! . . . the Holy Spirit will not emanate from our pores will not breathe our lips," waving the piece of paper in front of him, almost as if a signal to me.

"Christ must be INCARNATE in all men, all women — each and every one of us chosen as the Body named Jesus."

With the sound of those last words still hanging in the air, Tom took the few short steps up to the fireplace and, standing there a moment staring into the flames, threw the piece of paper onto the burning logs . . . "and a happy Amen to that forever!"

———————◆———————

"Forever" — the word coming from my mouth in a float of frozen breath, the sound of it waking me from a longheld stare to see my legs swinging, one then the other, out from the wall on which I still sit (how long?), the heels of my boots *thunk*-ing against the stones . . . wondering why I am not in sock-feet, how my shoes are back on.

Until the cold numbing comes through my pants and I lift my buttocks off of the wall and stand looking at the line of smoke rising from the hermitage chimney — the memory of it now slowly coming back.

Tom's words. . . ."Woman. The refusal. Fault in my chastity." Then, from his poetry about "M," "Recover *lost Zen breathing . . .* lose these *blue rhythms of despair*".

"What Zorba said was the only sin — to refuse a woman love," I say aloud, repeating my words to Tom as he threw my statement paper into the fireplace to end our discussion of his love experience with "M."

Over now, at last, *forever* — I tell myself as I trot back to the hermitage. Stay inside a while, a cup of hot tea to warm up, then take the camera and walk the woods where you and Tom had so often gone exploring for beauty.

Paddock fence at the edge of the woods where the photo journey
of author and Merton began.

All ready. Not much time left. Gotta hurry . . . as I close the
door behind me and hop off the porch, heading for the woods the
other side of the dark wooden racehorse fence that runs some fifty
yards out front to the right away from the hermitage. —Where Tom
and I would usually start our photo-journey and laughing run-on
poetry-read to each other, to ourselves, to any animals and all trees
and plants within earshot . . . the entire countryside target for our
lens-eye, and captive audience to our bardic yawk.

Only a few steps into the tangling brush, looking for the path
that winds its way to the small wood-step bridge over the wire
fence before reaching the first dirt road, I stop to straighten the
leather strap of the camera looped around my neck . . . and know
immediately that it will not be the same as when Tom was along to
guide and instruct me, endlessly finding and pointing out unique
objects of inspiration — found poems and paintings and sculptures
and music — all the time with a voice-over commentary and urging me on to the same . . . here now standing, twenty years later,
waiting for the sight and sound playback of those t   's Tao
wanderings when—

Monastery road leading to Merton's hermitage.

Tom would see me walking along in front of him and stopping to hold my camera to my eye, *snap*, then move quickly someplace else and *snap*, always turning my head around looking for something to *snap* again and again, here and there, almost anywhere.

"Stop! Stop . . . enough. You take more pictures in an hour than Ansel Adams (you know him?) takes in a month — maybe two or three a day, if you're lucky and *something finds you*! . . . Hold up a minute, let's try something, maybe talk about just what —"

And Tom would go on to teach me, when photographing (or any other time, for that matter) to stop *looking* and to begin *seeing*! — Because looking means that you already have something in mind for your eye to find; you've set out in search of your desired object and have closed off everything else presenting itself along the way. But seeing is being open and receptive to what comes to the eye; your vision total and not targeted. . . . The same holds for *listening* as opposed to *hearing*! —You can't approach sound or music already knowing or expecting what's to come, excluding all else surrounding it. That way you're making it do, not allowing it to be. . . . You can't appreciate anything around you if you're always self-conscious, thinking, blotting out everything else but you.

"Ron, you seem to carry the entire city inside you; it's there in your eyes. —Not that you should have the cow-eye look of now! as Rilke says . . . but you squint your vision, almost like you're focusing everything out there — separating, splitting apart the whole of it. . . . Accept things just as they are — just as you do with the wind against your cheek; you feel it right now, don't you? Don't say, 'It is windy'. . . what is the *it* that is *winding* you — other than the wind just being, not doing.

"And another thing while we're here," (once Tom was on a roll it wasn't easy to stop his rolling) — "keep in mind when you look through that little square of glass, you are the same as a sculptor eyeing a piece of stone, a painter surveying his canvas. All art is abstract, in that you arrange and select and balance the configuration of colors, shapes, objects so that it all fits into a mixed whole. And that's something to be especially aware of in photography — there's no particular thing at the exclusion of its field that you want to 'catch' as figure, as representation. Everything in that frame of light is 'essential' . . . nothing is primary, nothing is extraneous. . . . And once you know this, the photograph will show what you have seen. Believe me."

As usual, Tom was right about all this. And in a short time I was taking 'Zen photos' of weeds, limbs, rocks — all sorts of calligraphy. . . . And, now, I take very few pictures because I have to wait (just as in writing haiku) for *it* to present the image to me.

"That's what happens when I write — I can always hear the words in my head as they appear on the page. But with haiku I can see the entire poem before it's written," getting excited, telling Tom this. "It's like a quick eye-snapshot of it . . . with a 5-7-5 shutter speed for the three lines, seventeen syllables."

"Yeah, but . . ."

"I know, I know — haiku much longer in English," I came back, knowing Tom's thoughts about all this. "But I like to leave the lens open . . . to let more light in," smiling.

" Kind of fuzz the edges that way, eh?" —Tom letting me know that the image has to be sharp, minimal, clear.

"Empty, nothing — the poet. . . . Home, naked — a presence pointing nowhere," my voice quickly disappearing the issue.

"Ah yes . . . but—

> You must enter in
> To the small silence between
> The leaves

—what a very good friend once advised me," Tom now smiling.

"*Memento Mori* (be mindful of Death)"— the only speech once allowed the monks when encountering each other — all I had left to shut Tom down.

Which he did — folding his hands beneath his chin and bowing quietly . . . only to raise his head with a wide-eyed burst of breath, "Hai!". . . a wake up yell of light and Tom's face now a bright grin announcing *silence*.

———◆———

And I stand here in the woods, my feet seemingly stuck to this spot (for too many long minutes now). . . not getting anywhere. — This is not what I came out here to do. Get moving.

I cut back through the same path just made and come out of the brush, climb the fence, and head across the wide swath of deep grass to the woods on the other side. Here is where I need to begin. Just as Tom usually did . . . starting a zigzag striding hike through weeds and trees, up and down hills, crossing streams, hopping gullies, heading this way now that — his own *wu-wei wander* eventually finding our favorite 'song space' — a place I'm coming to now straight ahead.

Only a short climb to the top of this hill, trotting the last few yards to step into the shade of the low hanging branches of the tall pine tree. And here — the dry smooth wood of the large round log to plop down on, catch my breath, relax the searching, and just sit silent, looking out over the broad stretch of monastery land, and wait . . . a moment, another, and more . . . for the mind to clear, become empty.

And I'm 'back' once more (maybe the last) — where we'd rest, Tom and I, and "free ourselves to whatever enters as inspiration and exits as expression". . . those long meandering "word-outs" between two spirits caught in a wonder-web of give-and-take comments and questions about anything and everything, usually begun

On the way to the hermitage from the monastery building up into the woods.

with no more that a knowing shared glance, momentary contact of eyes that, with an assenting nod, linked our vision to "off on a talk," now books then ideas now artists . . . but seldom extensive drawn-out conversation of dialogue or discussion — just a clipped word or phrase or sentence here or there that "tinged our touch" and carried that special "think-mote" to hold the understood but unstated "learned baggage" that supported it — cryptic static bits of spark glinting our sight with lines of light. . . .

What I'm after here again now — but alone, with only the vision of memory unreeling behind my eyes . . .voicing a view of—

———————◆———————

Late morning and both of us finally settled, each sitting at opposite ends of the log. A few words exchanged earlier, then a long period of silence as we stared out over the land spreading green down and away along the valley to the horizon humping dark in the distance, the only sound a *whoosh* of wind gusting the tall pine branches above us or a lone crow *caw*-ing its glide at eye-level past the hilltop. Quiet, peaceful, contemplative . . . until—

"Eh, conflict between art and contemplation" — the words coming haltingly from my mouth. That *godawful problem* that I always accused Tom of creating for me. An issue that, after too many long years, he had come to terms with, but something that I could not quite shake . . . or at least forgive Tom for all the time I had wasted by not writing because of 'guilt' or some notion of 'spiritual compromise'.

At the sound of my voice Tom jerked his head back then up, his eyes scanning the sky, "Huh . . . wha . . . yes . . . who?"

I clunked the heel of my boot against the side of the log. "Cough. Cough . . . Hear the human being suffer."

"O Ron, it's you. I thought I heard someone gargling with language."

"Okay, okay. My ignorance growls in hunger. Are you going to feed my questions this morning?"

"No. You are," Tom said, pushing himself up from the log. "I expected something like this long before we left the hermitage, and I came prepared," unbuttoning the breast pocket of his work-shirt and pulling out a rolled sheet of teletype paper. "Something you had to say about all this some six or so months back — what you fed your poor trapped students."

"Hey, that's one of my letters. You said you burned all of those. Eh, we agreed."

"It's just a piece of a letter, and I will burn it, just like the rest. . . . But first let's experience the so-called "answer to your question."

"Aw, you're not going to make me listen to my own stuff being read again?"

"Exactly. It's what you want and what you need. . . . Now silence and attention for a few moments, please," Tom said as he unfurled the rolled sheet and held it in front of him, propping his right boot on top the log as he began—

What I wish to discuss here is the why and wherefore of human creativity . . . not in its most inclusive sense, to be sure, but in a context broad enough to include, however tentatively, the esthetic and philosophical dimensions — not to mention, at least generally, the spiritual realm out of which these dimensions emanate.

Creativity, in both the esthetic and cognitive processes, is basically a human attempt to realize transcendence within the confines and limits of the nature of existence.

Now, I wish to qualify the term "transcendence" so as to avoid all sorts of confusing and debatable understandings of the term and its meaning in the religious and spiritual sense. This is not to say that my subject and concern doesn't rightfully belong there; I just wish to appease, from the outset, the students of that particular academic or scholarly discipline, whether they be theologians per se or merely residents of that vaguely defined area of the humanities considered "religious studies". . . which, I would have to surmise, includes almost all sensitive, perceptive, thinking individuals among us — whether labeled anthropologists, sociologists, and especially humanistic psychologists (in all of their diverse schools of theory and therapy), and whoever or whatever else.

Having said that (however poorly or not at all) — I will now employ a well-worn term, bandied about as indiscriminately as an advertising slogan and, quite often (most seriously) restricted in its clinical sense to the allied fields of psychology and psychiatry, as well as, sad to say, 'pop-quackery':

Paranoia.

"Okay. Enough. I get the point. Cruel and unusual punishment, to say the least," I protested to Tom.

"No, I don't think you get the point. Not yet anyway. —Besides I'm just getting warmed up," Tom said, raising his arms above his head. "See the dark circles of inspiration."

And, switching feet atop the log, he leaned forward, rolled the paper a turn, raised his hand to *sssshhhh* my objections, and continued:

Groans from the regrettably trapped audience are recognized and humbly acknowledged.

But, to move forward.

After all, I'm indulging my vanity here. Each of you will have to justify your presence by whatever imaginative rationalization at your restricted disposal.

Paranoia.

The commonly understood and accepted meaning of the term in popular parlance (as well as Psych 101) is: an emotional malaise consisting of a *persecution complex* and *delusions of grandeur.*

Well, quite a "broad" (to say the least) category of the human race is defined and tagged here. In fact, to be quite honest, it appears to be as much a sweeping, all-embracing articulation of the state of human nature that consciousness allows. Who in this room [*on this hill!*] or anywhere else for that matter, if at all a reflective creature graced with the slightest modicum of courageous lucidity, is (guiltily or otherwise) umbrellaed by that definitive self-appraisal?

The human awareness of its condition as such is at the heart of tragedy (in the classical sense), as well as modernist existential *angst* . . . not to neglect these intellectually unfashionable, somewhat obsolete "victims" of introspective hypochondria (hardly welcome in the blue-collar salons of academe).

Ironically, this self-diagnosis and indictment (if you will) is the seed perpetually nurtured in the "enlightened" mentality of the *Mythers of Progress* — those *Agers of Reason* who are evolutionally molding (however gradually) the species' utopian Crystal Palace.

So, the contagion is upon us — no one excluded!

The diseased dark tentacles have reached the long insulated crevices of the human psyche.

Alas, the virus has discovered its original birthplace!

"A cure for verbal dysentery!" I moaned, falling to my knees and bowing my head between clasped hands. "A leper tongue has rot out these ears. Oh, forever silence this song of Babel."

"The chef must devour his own stew. Hear here the second helpings. Leftover bites of note," Tom announced solemnly as he stood rigid atop the log now his windswept pulpit, right arm extended and index finger jabbing the air with each point made:

"Persecution complex! . . . tragic enlightenment . . . fallen nature (original sin) . . . perennial problem of theodicy.

"Humankind is victimized — kicked out of Paradise . . . loss of innocence . . . alienated . . . estranged . . . homeless.

"Go back" by *escaping* human condition.

"How? . . . — transcendence!

"With what?

"Promethean myth of secular utopia! . . . Art! (natural mysticism of Gregor Samsa) . . . Religion! (by hurdling Freud and Feuerbach).

"All of the above — bankrupt!

"Which leads to the inevitable indictment: delusions of grandeur!"

Tom enunciating those last three words loudly as he stepped down off the log and, cocking his head sideways, said, "Whew! smell the change of wind — buffalo chips a-smoldering. If that's the way you spread it around as a pro-fess-or . . . the students'll be having an *auto da fé* in the college Merton Room."

Then he walked over and handed me the roll of paper. "Here, you burn it, eh," — his grin baring all of his teeth and pushing his cheeks up squinting his eyes.

I could only stand there holding my piece of writing, then look down at my boot moving back and forth in the dust, trying to figure out how Tom could answer my question by reading all of that back to me.

"Because one haiku is worth one hundred pages of that academic jargon you've got there," Tom said, as if he had been hearing my thoughts.

I folded the paper and quickly stuck it in my back pocket.

"You've heard the saying that 'Poetry is too fine for ideas' more than once, I know," Tom went on. "—Well, it's true. . . . Poetry is not trying to prove anything. It's not interested in converting or convincing anyone. It answers no questions, solves no problems. It does not teach — and doesn't care to."

Tom was standing directly in front of me, no more than three feet away, and now I had to look up and into his eyes.

"You asked me a question to be answered . . . something about art and contemplation, or somesuch. —And to do it the way you wanted, well that involved explaining and defining . . . and not experiencing! —which you get by making, not telling about."

Tom reached his arm out, his fingertips almost touching the front of my shirt, and, almost as if he were apologizing, said, "Ron, you've got to live the art . . . and live the contemplation . . . before you can talk about them, and that as an afterthought always."

I stood there looking at him, nodding my head in agreement to what he was saying, even though I wasn't quite sure I understood all of it.

"Oh, to be sure, reading philosophy and theology is fine, and we all do it. Even write it sometimes — a nightmare like my *Ascent to Truth*," Tom wrapping his palms across the top of his head as if squeezing it. . . . "But mostly, that's all an intellectual pastime like chess. Unless, of course, you've got some first-rate creative mind doing it. That's something else."

"Like all those you've been feeding me for years now — Kierkegaard, Nietzsche, Heidegger, Camus, the rest," I almost whispered. The first words I'd spoken in a long while.

"Yes, those. Plus all the great prose writers like Joyce, Proust, Faulkner . . . they're poets too. —In fact, any true writer is a poet. Right?"

"Sure. You bet," mimicking Tom's manner of speech.

The session ended — both of us smiling.

Back sitting on the log, we did spend time talking about the 'conflict' — the choice between art and contemplation — what it had wrought in our lives, the spiritual and creative energy spent and lost in the effort. We went at it in an indirect way — most of the input coming by way of tangential asides arrowing the target. The discussion coming to an abrupt end by Tom mocking a crow caw in the middle of a sentence — signal enough for me that we had entered a language tangle and couldn't (wouldn't) go any further with the subject.

We sat silent a long while. First Tom, then myself, got up and walked around, visited the evergreen bushes down to the left of the pine tree, did some knee bends, then came back to sit on the smooth wood of the log, look up at the sky and then out over the valley, before passing the bottle of water back and forth — just about ready to give speech another chance.

The give-and-take began slowly, our voices low and relaxed as the sun came and went behind the clouds gathering high above the wind gusting dust around us, everything even and steady until *something* — the air suddenly going gray as the blue in the sky closed all the way to the horizon darkening . . . or a sharp drop in temperature for a moment as rain briefly *splaat* the leaves behind us — triggered a change in our mood and tone of voice quickening to a sharper edge as we took off on a non-stop run of words covering everything expressed in a free association of ideas and feelings.

To begin: We had a good look at Tom and considered the very real possibility that he just might not be such a good monk or a true hermit because, first, he wasn't the ideal person for community and, second, he got too lonely to be a solitary. —The point about community was somewhat delicate with Tom in that he insisted upon a "true appreciation of the nature" of such . . . not an institutionalized housing of people, but "any gathering of loving people."

Which led to a discussion of the difference between loneliness and solitude — a contrast quite possibly the result of 'guilt'. Obviously not the so-called "guilt of wrongdoing" but, as with Kafka, "shame or embarrassment" for his *sin* (not so original) of suffering the separation or split (as we so often discussed). And Tom had come to the monastery to *cure* that — though not too shy in telling everyone about it. His admission: "What could I have done so poorly or wrong with my *Mountain* book that so many people would like it?". . . This not a smug statement but the genuine bewilderment of a poet — a question constantly with him, and a reminder of the *why* of his 'curative climb'.

Bringing us to the *how* of his so-called 'cure' — which involved renunciation! . . . First, by denying himself as an amicable, sociable, sensual, loving human being.

Asceticism his solution: to "*sacrifice* in solitude and silence any intimate touch with another person". . . to "mute the song of poesy and annihilate art!" —Both "home remedies a disaster of *denial*, but thank God not irreversible".

"Aw inevitable, Tom — the thing with "M". Something *spiritual* to come to terms with there, and you're a better person for it. Okay?"

And "Hey, your poetry has come full circle from your pre-monastery macaronic *Gestapo* book to your latest *Lograire* work. Both Joycean 'free and let-go of the apophatic lockjaw' — your true *say* all the while.

"*Lograire*? . . . O, your 'Country of the Imagination'. . . your 'Dreamscape Siqnature'. . . — just wondering."

Because at the same time Tom's writing his endless poembook *Geography of Lograire*, I have been writing my infinity-length millennium opus, *Bad Meat*.

And Tom now, having memorized the first two *Meat* lines, stood atop the log with arms spread and, in "affectionate ridicule," threw his head back and shouted loud to the heavens and anyone else within a county's radius of his lungs:

> so let it be across Whole Earth the endless hiccup
>   of yr High Priest I'm nervous
> circling the moon on broom with a hee hee cackle
>   laugh a wart on my nose

The echo of those pre-mortal words still stinging my ears as Tom sat back down — both of us laughing so hard that for several minutes we just let the talk rest.

But then those voiced lines served as a preface or purpose, really a sort of apologetics, for the title as well as the content of my poem *Bad Meat* . . . the sum of which I offered Tom as a compliment, and *complement*, to his *Lograire*:

"It seems that now, in the last two decades anyway, beginning really after World War II, but bursting out in the open during the 50s, the Beats and that entire revolution in art, especially poetry, the San Francisco Renaissance and the New York scene (of which I was at the center and only eighteen-nineteen years old), and on into the 60s with the so-called 'counter-culture' and everything that seemed to change forever how we perceived ourselves and the country as a whole, especially the political radicalism of the peace and civil rights movements, and, O hell, so much it's hard to talk about.

"Well, it seems, to me at least, that anyone who's even a bit sensitive or human at all, is left with a choice, two alternatives: either (for the purposes of security . . . physical or psychic survival) you plastic-wrap yourself for protection, deep-freeze yourself for preservation, or (and this is the position I take) you go out and live at the heart of it, expose yourself, be open and available and vulnerable, almost as a sacrificial martyr or, possibly victim or prey, as carrion-feast to the *Birds of Appetite* (familiar, eh?) . . . . that is, lay yourself bare at the risk of spoiling on the pavement — *Bad Meat!*"

After shouting my poem across the valley and a good laugh, Tom had sat there listening attentively to my "explication of the thrust of that long lament"— then replied that the entire thing sounded much like his "misanthropic ravings at the modern world" you find in *Tears of the Blind Lions* and *Figures for an Apocalypse*, two of his early books of poetry published not long after he entered the monastery.

"O that from 'the man who spurned New York, spat on Chicago, and tromped to Louisville, heading for the woods with Thoreau in one pocket, John of the Cross in another, and holding the Bible open to the Apocalypse!' . . . You see, I remember some of your stuff verbatim too."

But Tom had drifted off a bit, barely listening now — only to turn back quickly with, "Been thinking about what you said. That your long poem would not only compliment my *Lograire* but complement it . . . in that, as I read it, *Bad Meat* is, in actuality, a form of *ghost dance.*

"As you know, and is quite obvious, a major theme of my book, maybe even the essential part, is the Ghost Dance of the American Indians. The whole movement began around 1870 with the prophet Wowoka of the Paiutes in Nevada, and ended with the massacre of the Lakota up at Wounded Knee in 1890.

"You see, this was sort of a messianic cult arising out of desperation among the Indians. They could sense the inevitable demise of their entire culture . . . and realized that they were militarily, politically, and economically impotent . . . therefore unable by any means, other than Divine Intervention, to arrest the so-called Manifest Destiny of the dominant white culture to swallow them up.

"So, instructed by this vision of their prophet and passed on from tribe to tribe throughout the entire West — they did this ceremonial dance and sang these sacred songs as a sort of liturgy, a supplication to the Great Grandfather in the Sky (their name for God, what is it?). . . . Well — a last-ditch pathetic (but sympathetic, even empathetic for us) attempt to make the white man disappear, all the dead red ones to reappear, the millions of buffalo slaughtered to return, and the grass to grow green and high again over all the land. . . . A grand noble kind of prayer, really, to save the people, their culture and history and everything that it meant to be an Indian.

"But, as you can see, it was all magic! . . . a pitiful futile effort that, naturally, failed. The U.S. Cavalry blew the hell out of their invulnerable shields, the ghost-shirts they wore — and that was the end of their way of making things right again."

We sat silent a moment, then Tom said softly, "A good bet that is what all your pent-up anger and energy and creative effort is — the ancient Orphic and modern romantic ritual of verbal incantation, the poet as priest or shaman or unacknowledged legislator of the world who must act as the minister of salvation. . . . The enthusiastic undaunted hope of the young, the innocent, the trusting that things can be different — that their frustration, after being cheated in their expectancy of the Good, could be rectified by a revolution of consciousness. . . . It's what you see all around us now — the protest poets, the street music, the political activists, peace movement, civil rights. You know, Dylan, the Beatles, all the Beat writers, even some of that Hippie stuff. And I'm with them most of the time because of what they're against!"

None of which surprised me except that now and then Tom would become impatient with this so-called 'cultural revolution' and criticize its "adolescent excesses". . . all the drug-taking, the anti-rational stance, the "infantile spontaneity" of many of the artists, the attraction to all forms of the occult and anything that was "other than what we have here in this country or the entire western world"— why the rise in popularity of "cheap Eastern mysticism, instant Zen, guru groupies, destructive pacifists, all kinds of Jesus and Buddha freaks who haven't the patience or humility to live the longsuffering apprenticeship of spirituality."

And here Tom was more than adamant, standing and looking right at me, almost accusingly, "You don't go around mouthing the

Tzu brothers Lao and Chuang without paying your dues with the discipline of Confucius — all that Alan Watts casual Tao and Kerouac's drinking dharma. Good guys, no doubt, but Damn! it wouldn't do them any harm to take a look at D.T. Suzuki or Huang Po from time to time."

He picked up a small piece of quarry rock at his feet and threw it far down the hill. "And for God's sake, leave the poor American Indian alone. All of that romantic crap about the idyllic life of smoking peace pipes around a fire while the coyote sings to a full moon. —Whew! . . . at least give those people their due respect by at least knowing *something* about their very complex and oftentimes sophisticated culture and religious beliefs and practices."

Then calming, "Hell, every third day I get a letter from some distant great-cousin of Black Elk telling me that 'today is a good day to die' or somesuch solemn pronouncement I know uttered haltingly aloud in Indian movie-talk as it was written."

Both of us now smiling at the humorous spin he had put on the subject. Tom couldn't remain angry long because he knew all too well that the object of his railing was more often than not himself as much as anyone else.

"You know what Neitzsche said, don't you," I asked.

"Hell, Neitzsche said a lot of things."

"Madness. —He said the Germans, insufferably oppressed by being German, used Wagner like hash. . . . Madness, the perverse 'liberty' of people overwhelmed by giant forces of organized control," I said with a ring of authority in my voice, trying to hold my own. "Could be how many of us feel today in this country, and how we're reacting, eh?"

Tom looked at me with the beginning of that gleam in his eye when, out of a bunch of disconnected pieces, something whole had formed in his mind. "Yes,' maybe . . . you're probably right about all this, but — *can a ghost dance kill the rhinoceros?*"

"Wha. . ," I started to say, taken back by the force and suddenness of his question. Befuddled, too, by its meaning.

"No no. Not now. Sit on it for a while. Think about . . . until next time. Okay?"

Two long weeks to agree, okay, and we were back, the same place, sitting on the log atop the hill — but this time, early morning, surrounded by fog filling the valley to the front and sides of us, hunched to the damp air pressing through our thin denim work jackets.

"You know Han-shan . . . . his *Cold Mountain* poems?"

"Yeah. Yeah, I've seem em," faking it a little . . . interested in what Tom was going to say.

"They're good, very good. Clear, simple, right to the heart of it. —I know most of them, easy to remember, but especially the one . . . quite appropriate now," pausing. "Let's see, something like—

> Here we languish, a bunch of poor scholars,
> Battered by extremes of hunger and cold.
> Out of work, our only joy is poetry:
> Scribble, scribble, we wear out our brains.
> Who will read the works of such men?
> On that point you can save your sighs.
> We could inscribe our poems on biscuits
> And the homeless dogs wouldn't deign to nibble.

Silence. The fog seeming to absorb each word as it came from Tom's mouth. Both of us sitting there, looking straight ahead, knowing the *truth* of *Cold Mountain*.

Reminds me of another of your poems," Tom finally spoke. "Also too late for *Monks Pond* . . . but close to Han-shan here. —Do you remember the one I'm talking about?"

"Must be *On the Way Here*, right? You said something to that effect, then."

"You remember it now . . . the words, I mean?"

"Oh sure. The short ones, always. . . . Goes like this (I think)—

> so woke beneath the tall pine
> wondering about all that time passed
> & still not the poet
> to be—

some old Chinese	thin-whiskered
cold mountain haiku	
wintered to stone	in solitude
by rock & water	groopy

the final bare tree   of raining
gloom

last of the high-cheeked hermits
who opted for beauty

"Yes," Tom said.

And we sat silent again.

Until— "Hey, wait a minute now, Tom. You got me distracted, off the track of what you said I should sit on and think about. . . . the big question, *can a ghost dance kill the rhinoceros?*"

"Oh, that?"

"Yeah, that!—I've been thinking about it a lot since you mentioned it. All of what you said about the ghost dance, and that just maybe my writing the *Bad Meat* poem being just that: a futile waste of energy . . . more like a temper-tantrum reaction to the unquestionable authority of the ultimate father-figure for my generation — the established culture-in-residence."

"Something along those lines," Tom replied flatly (trying to give the impression of indifference to my agitation).

"Well, I went back and reread your *Rain and the Rhinoceros* closely, and it seems obvious to me your use of Ionesco's play as a symbolic expression of totalitarianism as opposed to the freedom of the rain . . . is what you're getting at with this ghost dance question. Right?"

"Hmm.That does sound familiar . . .even interesting."

"Yeah, sure," I glanced over to the side of Tom's face still turned to the valley in front of us. It was clear that he had made up his mind to listen, for the time being anyway, so I decided to go with it, giving him my well-worked thought-out response to his big question.

First of all, I told him, if you examined his concept of a ghost dance from the broadest perspective, it would have to include "all human endeavors to transcend mundane human existence"— that condition of existence implying the iron necessity of survival, or biological and all other forms of determinism: a definitive, absolutist premise arrived at by classical secular rationalism.

And (beginning to sound more and more the pedagogical fool-Prof that I was) went on to say that that *reality* was indeed our inescapable *rhinoceritis* — the curse or sin "made one with our nature."

And, furthermore, all human activity and so-called progress and achievements — including every scientific and technological theory and practice, every social and political and economic system, every religious and theological and philosophical school of thought, every expression and form of art (including our beloved poems and paintings and photography and music et al) . . . all institutions, all culture, all history in the end is nothing more than humankind's attempt to escape its fate — in a word, one big universal ghost dance!

"So, if you look at it that way, in its broadest terms, the answer to your question— Can a ghost dance kill the rhinoceros? —the answer is a resounding no, I say 'No,' again I say 'No!'". . . Long since having stood up, I was walking around, back and forth, flailing my arms histrionically as I articulated my erudition loquaciously and high-volumed . . . only to look over and see that Tom had rolled off the log and was lying on the ground with his head reared back and mouth wide open to loud snoring noises.

I walked over, kicked the heel of his boot a hard whack, and yelled, "Isn't that right, Tom?"

"Yes, yes. I agree with everything you've said. You couldn't be more correct. . . . *Harrumph! Harrumph!*" flashing his eyes wide open as if startled from a deep sleep.

"You lost the log-rolling contest once more. . . .Your last chance," I told him as he got to his feet, dusted off his pants, stretched, and sat back down on the log.

And I looked at him sitting there with a dark blue Navy toboggan cap pulled down over his ears, the stubble of graying whiskers on his unshaven chin, leaning forward with arms wrapped around his knees and one hand grabbing his other wrist, just staring out over the valley where the fog was lifting and the sun breaking the gray cloud cover eating the mist clinging to the tops of the pines lining the hills on our left. —And told myself: Tom is just another mountain-crag Han-shan hermit. A lone living poem waiting to get back to his hut and pencil and paper to scrawl his own 'little notices of nature'. Tom . . . a writer first and foremost, more at home with words than anything else. —Knowing this because, other than Sally and my boys, the same with me in my little cell bent to the page watching the pen in my hand loop the letters one-by-one on the clear, clean sheet.

And sitting there beside Tom then, I knew why and, more deeply, *who* I loved in him as I, unthinking, pulled my notebook and pen from my jacket pocket and, raising my eyes to the ever-green needled limbs of the tall pine tree appearing to float upward into the clouds, began "recording the vision" there before we arrived, there after we would leave—

> in the pine squeak cold
> the trees speak
>
> a creak of wood
>
> cracks its voice
> a freeze to night
>
> the black glints
> with snow
>
> footprints approach
> to leave
> this place
> of winter language
>
> the eye moving a pen
> across paper
> a blank white field
> of memory
>
> the voice unlistened
> no poem to mark it

The scratching of the pen stopped, Tom turned to me smiling and (as if no time had passed) said: "What you just said about the ghost dance and the rhinoceros. . . . some of that true, but took it too far, not what I meant. Especially about prayer, about poetry.

"The apocalyptic vision (if indeed there be one in ours) leads to the prophetic . . . through the purge of suffering comes joy (your old Janus-faced coin, eh?). So — does not end in pessimism. Just as it's not going to here, see," a grin widening to laughter.

"Talk, the poet says, is a form of love. Let us talk — at least that's what an old old friend once said," Tom announced with palms outstretched. . . . "You first."

Caught unprepared, I hesitated, searching. Then, "To write is to make the soul palpable. . . . I would not encourage that in anyone."

"Yours? —Not bad," Tom pressed his right forefinger to his temple. "But I'll start with Ikkyū:

> To write something and leave it behind us,
>   It is but a dream.
> When we awake we know
>   There is not even anyone to read it.

"How about your buddy, Picard? His 'Poetry is spoken music. . . . Prayer is a pouring of the word into silence'."

"Okay, but I'll stay with my Zen fools," Tom said tapping a small pebble off the top of my head. "Wake Up! . . . . 'There are three things I dislike: poems by a poet, handwriting by a calligrapher, and food by a cook!'. . .That's Ryōkan."

"Kierkegaard: 'State of the world and life is diseased. If a doctor and asked for advice, I'd reply: Create silence, bring men to silence'."

"You bring in heavyweights. Well — 'I always feel as though I stood naked for the fire of Almighty God to go through me. One has to be so terribly religious to be an artist.'. . . Surprise, D. H. Lawrence."

"Poetry is frozen prayer!"

"To breathe is to pray!"

"More human than Hamlet and Han-shan— I forgive myself! . . . Who said . . . Don't care. I give up too," crossing my arms.

"What about your buddy, road-bo Kerouac?"

"First thought, best thought!"

True, true," Tom added, slapping his thigh, laughing, "but in the end, must have something to say."

"Or, if you have something to say . . . be able to say it with words, especially if you're a poet, without biting your lips — even the thought of speech in this mute landscape hurting!"

"You talking about the great Minimal Mouth — my *Recording Angel Sent by God* — Bob Lax? . . . I'll chop off the finger who points such," Tom shouted.

"Or your Chilean anti-poet Parra. . . . *following his ecstasy . . .* tongue-tying the lyric knot. —The Charlie Chaplin of modern letters."

Tom jumping up, standing straight and pulling his cap off in a quick doff, replacing it cocked the side of his head, bowing stiffly in greeting, "Deliberate ironic feedback of cliche," speaking jacket-blurb, . . . "parody . . . a brutal satire of banality!"

"Why you wrote such lines as

> The red plague rid you
> for leaving me your language

in your *Ace Cables* . . . and why I refused to type that cemetery crow *caw caw*-ing the poem-grave of Early Tom choir songs!"

"Hey, my *Cables* no different from the *Meat* stuff you're writing — that long poetic retch!"

"Yeah, but I'm young and ignorant and impulsive — don't forget that! . . . and my sound reflects my jagged crack of contradiction."

"The whole point," Tom more serious now. "Your *say* is an expression of today's culture. . . . It represents the youth myth. — That's what anti-poetry is: reverse static or random noise by the new electric man."

"Electric . . . that a favorite word of yours throughout the *Cables*, and maybe why one of your favorite lines in my *Meat* poem. You remember—

> am I idiot to airy impulse
> jailing me electric in the prophet peep

—an excellent cluster of words, no doubt. You *do* recognize talent?"

"Yes, yes. By all means. My own especially, without scruple. But good J disturbed that apparently no one else does. With *Cables*, for sure; he's disappointed, surprised, really. Wait until *Lograire*, when/if he goes with that. . . . Even worse, I'm afraid. What will the great American poetry market do with my surreal nightmare mosaic writ full-blown in my new loon period?" —Tom grinning.

"Ah, answer to all this — your quandary, maybe mine soon too"— pulling my notebook out, flipping the pages in the back, running my finger down the lines scribbled hurriedly, until. . . "here: 'The lot of the man who has rebelled too much is to have no energy left except for disappointment.' —Hmm. No name, source . . . well," the book closed and back in my pocket.

"Aaggh!" Tom crossing both hands over his heart, "Once more felled by a quote apropos. . . . Whence come my next martyr-arrow?"

"From any random cricket short of his daily fool-quota."

"A most cruel curtain-closer of classic Noh play . . . you be."

"Time somone announce the fog-lift now sun-burst of light atop our heads, this hill, and all the land spread far below . . . ere time's up."

"Yes . . .true. Early morning over. Warming up. Enough time here musing in this Japanese landscape painting. Let the tiny, almost imperceptable figures leave the airy empty screen to the rock-crag scraggly-bush lone wisp-cloud-float in vast open space . . . disappear we must, and the void remain, still." —Tom quieting now, more serious. . . ."Return to bent-back labor of scribing in hut the veritable trace of our passing-thru."

But — knowing this possibly to be the last chance for a long while to spend time together at this special place, to talk of things spiritual (*essential* — to me, at least) . . . I asked Tom to wait a few minutes more, reminding him that my primary concern, the real reason for our returning up here was to talk out, hopefully to clear up once and for all, that major conflict (begun and ended years before with him, but still lingering not quite resolved for me) — a life of *contemplation* or a life of *art*: which one, or both, must I choose if I am to have a spiritual vocation?

And, realizing that he had written about this at length, explaining it all point-by-point in patient detail, giving it to me in manuscript to study long before publication — still it would help (and I *needed*) to hear his words face-to-face, assuring me again, in the simplest way, that there was no either-or choice to be made, that the two could be (and often were) one and the same.

So, with his back to the valley, sitting down to straddle the end of the log and face me still standing, Tom rested his arms across his knees and, gathering his thoughts, began, almost in a whisper to tell me, slowly — "In walking, just walk. . . . In sitting, just sit. . . . Above all — don't wobble."

And his laughter was echoing up and down the hillside long after we were gone.

———◆———

Alone. Sitting on the log. The feel of the smooth bare wood on my palms.

"Tom" —my voice sounding the complete silence surrounding me atop the hill.

Now my cheeks stinging cold in the wind. A flake of snow slanting past my eyes. Looking up to see the clouds clumped heavy and dark, a thick lowering cover spread over the entire sky all the way across the valley to the far line of black trees marking the horizon.

Not one bird in the tall pine tree rising just behind me. I bend over and pick up a small branch beside my boot and begin running my fingers down the long brown needles. Like the bristles of a Zen painter's brush.

My legs and back stiff as I stand, stretch my arms, start stomping my feet. How long have I been up here?

Get going. Back to the hermitage. A good distance, not much time . . . as I clomp my hard rubber soles against the smooth rock and begin clambering down the side of the hill.

Trotting on the flat clear stretches, brushing bushes as I skip around trees and hop ditches, now stepping long quick strides through heavy grass. The sun breaking through the dark gray clouds for a moment as I stop to pull the notebook from my jacket pocket and

> watching the sun make
> tree limb shadows on the snow—
> Zen calligraphy

scribbled across the page.

No more time for that . . . and I'm almost running now as I half-slide down the last hill and break out of the woods into the wide clearing of thick grass leading up to the hermitage. Just fifty yards more and *home* again as I hurry. Now close and

> neither bright nor dim,
> a light in the low window—
> simply so, his hut

scribed in my mind as I approach the porch, stepping up to see the faint glimmer of log ashes lighting the pane of glass orange against the closing dusk.

I stop at the door and, before entering, reach up to the corner of the roof and wrap my bare hand around

> a careless touch and
> broken beauty at his feet—
> fallen icicle

written carefully on the blank sheet before stepping into the front room of the hermitage still warm from the dim glow of the fireplace.

A few minutes to rest up, shake the chill off, heat the water and cut a wedge of cheese while the bubbles boil in the pot, dipping the small bag up and down in the mug now filled dark and hot to my lips as I walk over to the desk, sit down, open the notebook once more and, bending to the page . . .

> a cup of warm tea
> and time enough for writing—
> easy the haiku

Now twenty-five years writing them, "Always think that way," I once told Tom. "Words appear various places time-to-time. Little Zen ink poems. Simple poor voiceless say to Life. No 'I' —just AM, anonymous."—To which he replied, "Well, if that's the case . . . your new name now Hai-kū!"

Sitting here, alone in the hermitage, arms resting on Tom's desk, looking out his window — talking to myself now. Something to fill this emptiness.

My flat stare broken by the snow-muffled tolls of the monastery bells. Four o'clock. —My longday visit here closing fast.

Again I see the light behind me reflecting my face in the glass. And listening to the echo of the last bell fade into the gray air of all that out there (waving my hand across the wide window), I turn the chair around to

> Gethsemani bells.
> Firelight on his rocking chair.
> —twenty years ago?

And know that it is time to leave, be up and out of here.

So, one last check to see that everything is in order. "Always leave a place better than you found it," Tom had told me years ago.

Jacket on, buttoned up tight. Notebook and pen in pocket. I pull the door closed behind me, lock it with the key provided, push the screendoor tight, and take three steps to jump off the front edge of the porch . . . but stop.

I place the palm of my right hand high up against the rough wood of the porch post and listen. A crackling sound alongside the hermitage.

Leaning out over the edge of the porch and looking up, I see a thin line of smoke still drifting across the roof and through the limbs of a tree next to the outside wall of the chapel.

A good sound. Clean enough to close my eyes:

> with slow-motion drop of ice
> from trees
> the brittle crystal world
> melts away
> its zero clear freeze
> of water
> and slides crackling
> off limbs
> to scatter the ground
> with broken rain
>
> its icicle now
> cold wet pieces
> of winter

wind reddening my cheeks as I stand a moment, silent, before turning to see the firewood stacked below the window and one of the small wooden meditation benches sitting there a few feet from me.

O the poetry here! Always. What Tom shared with me. A place to pray to those black limbs high in the tree outside this hermitage:

> In your moving, Bless Me
>
> Holy I am the Wind
> blowing leaves
> bending weeds
>
> That dry scratching sing
> of Winter
>
>   My Name

Meditation chair on front porch of Merton's hermitage.

As I stand here leaning my shoulder against the porch post, staring out over the dimming bottom lands. Time enough for one more remembrance — of our last time together.

. When Tom had written . . .

———————◆———————

Typed on the inside of a small folding card — a photograph (Tom's) of the top of the wooden cross in front of the hermitage rising above a mound of trees in the distance and a bank of mist and clouds for beyond that: a stark black and white image surrounded by, almost floating in, a wide expanse of empty space . . . an oriental landscape painting.

Tom's brief note requesting a ride into Louisville for his trip to the Far East—

Sept 3   Gethsemani

Dear Ron:
Thanks a lot. Next Tuesday will be the final
trip out-- I hope. Taking plane next a.m. at
8. I need to go to St Matthews and then to
Tommies -- and can get to Fr John's eventually.
Maybe if you could come slightly earlier -
I have to stop off in Bardstown and get
something at the health dept. But 11 is still
ok.10.30 even better. Plenty of time.
                Best always,

                    Tom.

On a cool morning in early September 1968, I arrived at the Abbey of Gethsemani. It was around nine o'clock, too late to accept Tom's invitation to celebrate a farewell Mass at the hermitage. By the time I pulled my station wagon up to the frontporch, Tom was almost finished packing and putting his remaining belongings in order.

After the suitcases were in the back of the wagon, he generously loaded me up with things that he wouldn't be needing then, going on a trip, or later, when he returned — books and literary magazines from poets and publishers all over the world, and a healthy stack of record albums (mostly jazz . . . a few of which I played just last night to help me better remember).

"Here, take this and wear it," Tom said, pushing a large black felt western hat onto my head. "Came from a southern preacher who's been working with the Klan . . . a friend of Faulkner's." —the most precious gift.

He stuffed the camera, that John Howard Griffin had given him, into the last bag, a small tote, which I put on the front seat between us. Then we walked around inside the hermitage, checking the clean bare look of it . . . a Virgin Mary ikon on the wall. The hanging Suzuki calligraphy scroll. His desk cleared, with only a typewriter now. The empty rocking chair beside the fireplace. Not much else.

Tom stood silent a moment in the center of the large front room. Then, with a wave of the hand towards the back rooms, "Already checked them. . . . All clear," he turned and walked out the door.

We shook hands goodbye to the young Brother who had been helping Tom prepare for his journey. I started the car and pulled a few yards away from the porch, holding the door open for Tom . . . waiting.

But he had stopped a few feet from the hermitage and stood on the grass now, looking. Surveying one last time this place that had held his silence, his solitude. This little prayer-hut that has been 'chosen' as a holy spot, a *sacred space* for his life of contemplation, his *enclosure.* —Then he quickly climbed in the frontseat and we drove away, neither of us looking back.

Reaching the end of the dirt road, Tom got out of the car to swing the wide iron gate open for me to drive through. Then closing it again, his hands held onto the top bar a moment and he slowly moved his eyes over the short shallow valley on up to the Abbey Church and the rest of the monastery atop the hill.

"Say goodbye, Tom," I shouted, leaning out the window.

He raised his arm, "Hai!", and turned away. Getting back in the frontseat, laughing, "Heck, they won't even know I'm gone, or care, before I'm back. . . . Good riddance! 's what they're saying."

—(Actually, only three monks and the Abbot were aware that he was leaving.)

Once again we were making the long drive to Louisville — the last one for some time I knew then, thinking about the far journey ahead of him the coming months.

We stopped briefly on the outskirts of Bardstown, a final check with the Health Department to see that everything was in order. And pulling back out into traffic, I decided to take the old Bardstown Road route — a winding two-lane highway that was much more interesting and scenic (with enough beer-and-sandwich small taverns every few miles to make the drive enjoyable), but dangerous too because of the many farmers unexpectedly pulling onto the road from behind one of their corn-rolls or fruit orchards. This way would take much more time, and that's what I was after.

Time enough to spend a few extra hours with Tom. To remember, talk, and laugh about so many things in our lives the past ten years. People, places, and experiences that then seemed almost eternal — in that the interest, energy, and enthusiasm of the moment was at its peak, so full and shimmering with life . . . how could it ever *not* be!

One of the main reasons Tom was excited about going into town was to see Dan Walsh before leaving. It had been a long time now and we began talking about Dan.

—About how he was *the* teacher for both of us. Dan telling me that Tom was "so impatient as a student and now the same as a teacher (of the novices)." And Dan telling Tom the same of me, "be a good teacher someday in spite of being so impatient and expecting so much . . . unable to *instruct*." Both of us laughing because that is exactly why Dan was good: he was not an instructor but someone whose presence was "the spirit of inquiry, the creative climate of questioning." He was a vital, dynamic, living thinker, not interested in "dead thoughts." Telling us instead that "Wisdom is the experience of unknowing!" That, as students, we were very intelligent but not informed (little knowledge, less education); "wit, humor, irony, satire . . . oh yes, that! . . . but wisdom, not a bit" — and why and how the two of us relate so well.

We talked about how Dan tried to teach us to *be anonymous!* Have no personality for people to know. As a teacher "become who and what you teach." —and that's exactly what he did. Tom and I agreed that that had been our experience: we came away each day from his class living the Truth! . . . not dying of information. That's what Dan's Philosophy of Person was all about — a shared realization of what made each of us a *who* and brought us together into *one* . . . and not separate or split us apart by making each of us *unique* as individuals!

Thinking of that silenced us. —But not for long.

We went on to talk about the many other sides of Dan Walsh. Of how he was a close friend of the Kennedys and was invited to address both Houses of Congress one Christmas. And that, in fact, he was a godfather to one of Robert Kennedy's children, just as he was to my second son, Sean Merton, named after Tom. How I used to monitor his final exams at the College and then mail the papers to him down at the Kennedy home in Palm Beach in Florida, where once, while correcting them, he dropped the whole pile of blue notebooks into the pool and had to give everyone A for the course.

Both of us laughing now as I told Tom of my taking Dan to the Archbishop twice a week for instructions when he was about to become a priest —how he had reprimanded me more than once after lunch for laughing and talking too loud in the presence of such a holy man. . . . And later, at his ordination party at Tommie O'Callaghan's, how he introduced me to a prominent critic or publisher from New York and told the man that Tom Merton had said that I was "the best young poet in the United States," then walked away quickly with me standing with this stranger, both of us not knowing what to say.

And oh, the gifts Dan would shower on me. Sausage and bread and monastery cheese sometimes three times a week — all of that smelly cheese piling up and even too much to give away to enemies. Tom laughing, "Yeah, but with you and Sally, three babies in as many years—a good, and approved, method of birth control . . . so long as only one of you eats it."

Which reminded Tom of the monastery gift shop where Dan purchased all of "that baroque and rococo holy junk jewelry of medals and kitsch crap church souvenirs to press into people's palms with a pious bow of 'Bless you, child'"—ah sincere and well-meaning Tom knew, but no taste or patience for it.

All of the Dan talk ending with Tom reminding me though of the "essential goodness of the man" —the person who had once told him years ago, as a young man before the monastery, that, "Even if the whole dike of goodness were collapsing under the weight and pressure of increasing evil . . . do not run to save yourself, but stand your ground and keep your one small finger in that hole in the dike — that is the meaning of hope."

True, true . . . nodding agreement as we slowed through a small town, then sped-up again, getting closer to Louisville — the rest of the trip spent reminding Tom of all the "wild goose chases" he had sent me on with inexhaustibly diverse interests:

—a full two weeks of my valuable time researching the blues for one of his 'works-in-mind';

—another month of searching all of Louisville for "someone who's into Sufi . . . check out the Black Muslims";

—weekends checking all the libraries for "anything and everything you can dig up on the Kennedy assassination";

—visiting all the bookstores to buy (pay me later) "all the Beat books you can find in print";

—reading all of Mailer's political essays and books to "see if they're worth looking into";

—listening attentively (excited and believing) as he told me of his plans to "work with the Klan . . . a real challenge";

—the same with his intention to "join Cardenal and the guerrillas fighting for social justice in South America";

—telling him of poet Ferlinghetti's cabin at Big Sur, a place to stay when he traveled West, where Kerouac wrote his last novel (something that he'd check out);

—giving him my new book of Henry Miller-Lawrence Durrell letters to read on the plane (a lot of literature he'd have to catch up on);

—recalling his directions for me to pick up John Howard Griffin at a *Black Like Me* lecture at Memorial Auditorium in Louisville (three hours long and, afterwards in the lobby, rescuing John from a swarm of sisters and Sisters surrounding him);

—meeting Brother Antoninus, the Dominican west coast mad monk-poet, and attending his "poetry-reading" where he stomped his size 14 shoes around in a circle for half-an-hour before letting out a deranged scream and throwing a pitcher of drinking-water into the audience . . . the next day driving him around to satisfy his obsession to "find that Kentucky bluegrass" before bringing his almost seven foot tall prophet-hulk to the hermitage after a fifteen-year-long wait to "just sit down and talk a bit with Merton";

—and this and that, one and another and more, on and on. . . .

Now nearing the city, I turned off and headed towards St. Matthew's, a small suburb where Tom had to visit his doctor. He was laughing so hard at the "valet's hardship litany" that I had just laid on him —we had to sit in front of the office until his "vital signs regular."

In a half hour we were heading for my home and a short visit with lunch. Tom was settled again, relaxed after the Doctor's check-up, and he was telling me about the poet Zukovsky, . . . about the "paradise ear."

"The poet has this curiosity about words, the way a child does. Children's language is the language of paradise. Conversation with a child is not baby talk, not by any means. To talk like a child is to say words for the first time! —It's to discover language all over again."

I told him I couldn't agree more. My three sons were a good example of what he was saying. "You want to hear some really good poems?" I asked him.

"Sure . . . long as they're not yours," grinning.

"Here's one that Dylan, my oldest, came up with recently. Only five years old but . . . knocked me over with this:

> (HE)— "It's embarrassing."
> (ME)— "What's embarrassing?"
> (HE)— "It's spring
> and it's snowing on the flowers."

"Great. . . . See. See what I mean?"

"Wait. Here's another. . . . Sean, the next one, four years old:

    (HE)—   "That's a fossil."
    (ME)— "Well, what is a fossil?"
    (HE)—   "A fish whisker in stone."

"Right," Tom said, "Couldn't be more simple, concrete."

"Just one more. Casey, my youngest, three years old. —He didn't voice this poem. . . . It was the pure innocent (unthinking) gesture. Tao? . . . that I recorded, put into words:

    Casey came forth   Good Friday
    a dandelion cupped   dead
    in his hands
                a chalice
    for Sally

Tom cupped his hands below his chin, nodded — smiling silence.

"You said you didn't want to hear any of my poems. Can't blame you. But, there *is* one . . . and maybe not the language of children — maybe not *that* innocent — but . . . paradise . . . I think maybe so," pulling the car over to the curb about a block from home. "You liked it. More than any of my others, you said. —It's about Sally . . . one of the first times I saw her." Then looking at Tom, "Maybe it touched something you experienced with 'M', eh? I said. —And once more, softly, moved my lips to:

    as you lean to the wood, writing
    your hair falls
        hanging in space
    and each movement of the pencil point
        swings the dark lock, its shine

    and I am weaker because
    the heavy walls of my cage
        give way
        come crumbling down
    as a glacier wall does when

the ice, cracked
slowly lets go its hold
and falls crashing, white
a broken island
sinking, then gone
to the watery bottom
that is myself, truly

when beauty enters me

By the time we arrived, the whole family was a little nervous, having waited for over an hour, anxious to see Tom again. He gave Sally a big wrap-around hug "Hello"— then took each of the three boys in turn, sat them on his knee . . . talking and laughing the innocent speech of children, and poets.

I began unpacking the car, bringing the books and records in and placing them on the livingroom mantel.

Tom had taken the boys out in the backyard. He played with them a long time — running around, chasing and catching and rolling them in the grass.

Sally called us for lunch. Something simple Tom had insisted — so just a sandwich, fruit, and iced tea.

After a short prayer of thanksgiving, everyone sat around the table, the boys on both sides of Tom. But before he could take his first bite, I said: "Hold it. . . . Got to have music to eat by. Just as you always say, Tom." And I pulled out one of his albums and placed it on the phonograph there in the dining room. "Now listen to this, everyone — Tom's favorite."

It was Jimmy Smith and his organ. A funky blues-jazz rendition of "Got My Mojo Workin."

And on hearing the first note, Tom got up from the table and started a sort of shuffle dance, singing along, bobbing his head up and down — his own kind of 'Monk's Boogie'.

"Mojo! Mojo!" he kept repeating with Jimmy Smith. All the while grinning as the boys laughed and clapped, until he waved his arms for them to "Come on . . . join in."

Which they did — hopping off their chairs and jumping around him in a circle, yelling "Mojo! Mojo!" and grabbing his hands. Some kind of whirling-dervish dance that had all of us joyously 'letting go'.

"Tried it in New York City . . . gonna try it out on you," Tom sang, pointing at the boys. "Sprinkle you with goober dust," his eyes wide and a whistle following.

All of it ending with every one of us standing there laughing and clapping. —And afterwards, me trying to explain to the boys just what a *mojo* was: simply some kind of voodoo magic love charm . . . "Ask Muddy Waters sometime."

Then, after eating, there was the hugging, kissing goodbyes to Sally and the boys (Dylan, Sean, Casey). They were all standing on the front porch, waving.

And we were off again, to buy some supplies for Tom's trip.

We went to a large discount department store and rummaged among workpants, boots, ponchos, and the rest. Trying on big hats in front of mirrors, cartoon foolery, laughing at each other. Until we finally picked out a long hunting jacket, much too large but to Tom's liking . . . pockets all over the place.

"This pocket here for my camera. These two for my notebooks. This one back here for my bottle of wine. Let's see — fill this one with grapes and cheese in case I get hungry wandering around in those Himalayas."

"And that little bitty one there on the side . . . Save that for your mojo."

Both of us now wound up, laughing little Zen quips:

"Han-shan giggles. . . ."

"In our ploop haiku. . . ."

"Shamble signatures."

To fire a bouncing-ball duo singalong:

"The holy indifference of innocents. . . ."

"Let loose in paradise play—"

"Grins so wide with poemed paradox. . . ."

"You'd think St. Francis slapstick. . . ."

"In his stigmata—"

"Not a cloud-wisp of tracery. . . ."

"In our passing thru—"

as Tom stood in the middle of the store, turning around, modeling that huge hunting jacket for me and all heaven to see.

Then going through the cashier checkout lane, unaccustomed to having money (much less buying anything), Tom pulled out a bulging roll of bills and dumped the entire amount on the counter (his whole bankroll to get him to the Far East) . . . all the time humming (for my benefit), "Buy buy buy, gotta buy buy buy"—an innocent, very funny (to me) gesture that totally nonplussed the lady cashier.

And after asking how much he owed, Tom began sorting through the piled bills until he came up with the right amount, then scooped up the remaining 'change' and stuffed it into one of the large pockets of the jacket. He wore it right out of the store, handing me his old jacket, saying: "Here, you can have this. It's still good."

And it was — as good and stylish as one could expect of an olive-drab monk's going-to-the-city wardrobe.

"Thanks. . . . I'll save it for special occasions. Solemn High Masses and such," I said, getting into the car.

Now a list brief visit to the Merton Studies Center. A small room the back of the library, housing all of the materials (his manuscripts, photographs, drawings, etc.) that Tom had willed Bellarmine College a few years back. The custodian there always had a tough time deciphering his pinched European script, so he spent a half hour or more checking names in various correspondence.

A little embarrassed already, I think about the concerned scholarship surrounding his work, Tom had to make a joke about the Merton Room: "Let's get the hell out of here . . . It's a good place to cut a fart and run."

In a hurry then, we drove up the campus road to see our good friend Father John Loftus, longtime Dean of the College, who only late in life had come to appreciate Tom's vision and was the person responsible for the Merton Center.

Father John was in his room, quite ill at the time. He was very happy to see Tom and say goodbye. But the meeting was strained. Both men alike in many ways — John, so much wanting to express his affection and gratitude, but the silent interior kind of person unable to do so. I felt such an intruder as they stood facing each other, hardly speaking. John's eyes began to fill as he shook hands farewell, and I turned and left the room.

It was time for Tom to take a break, get some rest, and be ready for the final get-together dinner with several of his closest friends in Louisville.

A few minutes past seven o'clock and we were all there. A place called the Pine Room, away from town out River Road, sitting high on a bank overlooking the Ohio. It was a nightspot restaurant, maybe a bit too conventional and formal for Tom's tastes. As we were being seated in the large dining area at the rear, I remember him surveying the room, noticing the plush red velvet baroque decor and, aside to me smiling, "This place looks like a French bordello — are you sure we're in the right place?"

Tom's last night here before he left on his long-awaited trip to the Far East. Surrounded by people who had a special feeling about him, a deep affection and respect (some would even admit love), who were anxious about his leaving and would miss him more than he could know: Dan Walsh, Frank and Tommie O'Callaghan, Jim Wygal and Beatrice, Sally and myself . . . a few others. —An awkward situation for everyone.

The atmosphere of the dinner was tense. And several of us, trying to mute our emotions, didn't hold up too well. This especially sad because of the uniqueness of the occasion. —Enough to say that it was a difficult, traumatic experience for most . . . and I'll leave it at that.

After the dinner, after one toast and two and three, and after saying farewell with a handshake, an embrace, a kiss to each of his friends in turn — Tom left with a wide sweeping wave of his hand and a smile to the group standing huddled together there outside in the dark, a light rain beginning to fall.

He got in the car with Sally and me for the drive back to Lenihan Hall on the hill above Bellarmine College, where he would spend the night in a room close to Father John's.

It was really raining now and, with all three of us sitting in the front seat, Sally in the middle, we drove a short way out River Road, turned right, then wound our way along the wet shining curves of Wolf Pen Branch Road. And with the rain beating so hard against the windshield that we could hardly see, Tom began to loosen up some again after the uncomfortable pressure of the evening. He leaned forward in the seat talking excitedly about his departure in the morning and the long journey ahead of him. For months out at the hermitage he had been poring over travel books and maps of the countries he was going to visit, and now, finally, he was just a few hours away from the realization of those long plans.

We started joking about how one of those snakes was going to get him over in India.

"Might not be as slow as that one in your outhouse," I said. Then added (in jest but, now, thinking back, maybe a little fearful then), "You won't be coming back here, Tom. You're gonna disappear in one of those jungles over there . . . and all they'll ever find of you is a little wooden cross marking your grave."

The thought not so humorous to Sally, but Tom laughing, "That's all right with me. Wouldn't be a bad way to go. —But that snake just might not bother to put up a cross when he's finished."

A slow half hour drive and near the College now, Sally and I began talking about our European trip four years before. How we had planned to make the island Majorca in Spain our base from which to travel the length of Europe, visiting all of the poets and philosophers and artists on the list that Tom had made up for us before we left. And I was to write big novels in a cheap pension overlooking the Mediterranean — some kind of Fitzgerald-Hemingway romantic dream that I had been nurturing for ten years.

All of it to come crashing down when baby Dylan (ten months old) got dysentery in Madrid, and Sally (four months pregnant with Sean) got bounced from her seat onto the floor of a bus as we careened through the streets of Barcelona. The trip one big self-indulgent fiasco (on my part) that ended with us flying straight back to the States, stopping in New York, only to continue on to further misadventures in Hollywood.

What I'm coming to here is what I reminded Tom of then, riding home in the rain. . . . When we finally did get back to Kentucky and out to Gethsemani to tell him of our 'adventure abroad', of all the pathos and near tragedy of it —he laughed, slapping his knee: "What a glorious experience!" . . . . meaning (I now know), how enriching it was for us in terms of wisdom gained through all our suffering. But, at the time, I felt like punching him right in his paunch for such a response to our harrowing tale of near disaster and shattered dreams.

"So don't you come back here in a few months with any sad stories, or you'll get the same sympathy. . . . I'll play the Zen Master this time," I told him as we pulled up to his place atop the hill at the college.

And goodnight.

I would see him early in the morning — six o'clock. Plenty of time to catch his plane out.

Not yet dawn, the rain ended now and the pavement dry, I drove up the long steep road as the night before and parked atop the hill in front of Bellarmine's Lenihan Hall. Again at the fateful place of Tom's last meeting with his good friend John Loftus. And, saddened by their awkward farewell, I just sat in the car, (at the exact space where in three months, another midnight rain, Dan Walsh would collapse in tears at the thought of Tom's death that very morning).

The yellow light shone through the closed blinds of Tom's large window and I stared a long time at the glass square before grabbing a sheet of paper off the front seat and sticking it in my jacket pocket as I slammed the door behind me and walked through the wet grass in the dark.

The hallway was very quiet. I stood in front of his door, listening, then tapped my knuckles three times against the wood, and waited. Nervous now, but raising my hand to knock again, the doorknob slowly turned and a crack of light opened to Tom's face grinning a nod of *Well, good morning, come in, come in.*

"Hey, a little early, eh?" Tom *ssshhing* me with a finger to his lips. "These guys not monks. Don't want to wake them."

"It's okay, been here lots of time, walls're thick, can't hear anything," I said, closing the door behind me, standing just inside the room, embarrassed to be there.

"Almost ready," Tom whispered over his shoulder, walking away. "Make yourself comfortable. Got plenty time."

"I know. Why I came early," I said, raising my voice, still nervous. "Wanted to talk about something before you left."

Tom was sitting on the edge of the bed, bent over tying his shoes. "Sure, sure. No problem. . . . You don't mind our talking while I finish getting my things together, eh?"

"Yeah. I mean, no. . . . I just wanted you to know that *The Way of Chuang Tzu* is your best book. Really, your true autobiography . . . Much better than *Seven Storey Mountain*," I said, sitting quickly in the nearest chair (about five feet from Tom) — my face flushing hot at the sound of my awkward words.

Tom looking up, "Yeah. Dan told me you said that." Smiling, "Made me feel good. . . . That's how I feel about it too, but didn't want to say because of the 'Eastern thing' you know." Lowering his voice, "Lots of people might not understand, eh."

"Right, probably so," mumbled into my jacket collar. "But that's really not what I came to talk about. . . . Well, maybe has something to do with it, indirectly," I said, pulling the sheet of paper out of my pocket. "It's got to do with what I've been questioning you about the last few years. You know . . . ever since that day I came out to the hermitage to ask what you thought of my novel, the one about my big childhood crisis with religion and Christianity, historical Jesus and all that . . . when I really went off, yelling all of that ignorant trash, mad as hell at everything and everybody."

Tom was standing now, looking at me intently as I talked. "Well, I've been thinking it over ever since, seriously. And I've come up with this . . . as a sort of preface to the book," handing Tom the sheet of paper.

He picked up his glasses from the small table beside the bed and, holding the paper in front of him, glanced at me quickly, then looked down and began reading:

> And I, too, one of the sophisticates purged of my medieval ignorance, bearing the unwelcome scars of radical theology, carry with me the pulse, however faint sometimes, of that life blood pumped hot and red into me when first I opened myself as a child to what Rome, the Pope, Father Fear and Sister Guilt, and my good shoulder-riding Guardian Angel offered to 'save me with'.
>
> And I'm not sorry for it. I must never hate or be ashamed of that part of me. But I must get to know it. I must learn to love it for what it is.
>
> And I can only do that by touching it . . . not in apology, not in analysis . . . but in the concrete, by experience. If only through art, in poetry.

"Good. That's good . . . maybe take care of the problem for you," Tom said slowly, turning and placing the paper on the bed. "Even though I don't think your novel needs that kind of explanation or whathaveyou. What you say here," waving his hand, "is already *there* . . . in the book. Just as you say — in the concrete, in poetry."

He had taken his glasses off again and now sat on the edge of the bed with both hands clasping his knees spread wide to his shoes flat against the floor — his clear eyes unblinking, locked to mine.

I could not hold the stare. Moving my eyes to the paper lying on the bed beside him, motioning my hand to it, I said, "In my journal, about seventy pages, I've written . . . trying to straighten out in my own mind just what I think about the absolute essentials of the Christian faith. And I don't think there are any problems for me anymore — at least in the mystical sense . . . whatever that might mean."

I turned away, facing the wall. "But I have to admit being more at home with Buddhism, Vedanta, Zen, the Tao, and much else that makes up Eastern spirituality. So . . . I guess there still is a 'problem' of my getting the two together."

Tom was up again, walking across the room to stand in front of a mirror, adjusting his Roman collar. "What time is it?"

"Eh, ten . . . almost quarter after six."

"Well, just got to put a few of these folders in my briefcase, check my coat and pants pockets to see if I've forgotten anything." Turning his head quickly, "Yeah, my little cap here. My pen and notebook. . . . And I guess that about does it," patting the side of his jacket. —"Whoa! the airline tickets," sliding the packet off the bedside table and sticking it in his inside coat pocket.

"I'll start taking your luggage out to the car," I said, relieved to be going, trying to erase what was on the paper and all the loose talk rambling unintelligibly from my mouth.

"Naw, hold up now, Ron. . . . We've still got some time — about fifteen minutes," Tom said, motioning for me to sit down. We've been through some, maybe most, of this before, but we won't be seeing each other for a while. . . . Maybe we can take another quick look at this thing, this problem — if there really is one — and come up with something that'll work for us, at least until I get back . . . More time and all, then. Okay?"

I sat in the small chair beside the door, my hands gripped tightly around my knees, looking up to that longtime now friendly face once again about to try, with patience, to offer some kind of peace to a proud, but troubled soul.

"First thing, keep in mind that some of the words — often the really important ones — can be substituted by other words meaning basically the same thing in many different spiritual traditions. . . . That's important to remember here — especially for you and this Eastern thing, eh?

"Alright now," Tom said, clasping his palms together and taking a few steps towards the window, his back to me. He stood there silent a few moments, then dropped his hands to his sides and turned around. He looked at me directly, but in a very relaxed gentle way (unlike his usual intense, almost open stare), and softly, slowly . . . (as best as I can 'catch it' in memory) . . . said:

"You know, if God is really *here*, in this room, in this place — as we know he is, eh . . . we can't be in too much trouble, now can we?

"See. Either we are one with the Holy Spirit, or not. Eh? And if the incarnation, the 'Word Made Flesh', is a living reality — then the whole cosmos is sacramentalized . . . is sacred and holy . . . is redeemed. —Is really Church, see [smiling] . . . and you can't get out, eh, can't escape that . . . even if you wanted to.

"So, you see, you don't really need to get anywhere or be anybody — all that so-called ambition and 'going somewhere' thing . . . you're already who you are and where you are: home! . . . really — God's house, eh? . . . Creation.

"Now—as we've said so many times before — you've got to stop all this stuff about just-i-fi-ca-tion. . . . Let go and be who you have always been! —That's the one-time, most important thing you've got to remember to remember. That's the true meaning of *resurrection* . . . a return to your original source. —Go home to God.

"So — again I want to remind you — stop trying to be other than who you are by erecting monuments of your achievements — such things as books, artworks, great ideas . . . you know: evidence to prove your worth and justify your existence to God. —That's all so much waste.

"See. That's the true meaning of *hope* . . . to trust in the ultimate goodness of creation. —Hope doesn't mean an anticipation or expectation of a deliverance from an intolerable or oppressive situation or condition. . . . That's what most of us are doing most of the time: wanting something other than what is. As I said — true hope is trusting that what we have, where we are, and who we are is more than enough for us as creatures of God.

"To appreciate this, you've got to know that *revelation* is all around you all the time. —Revelation expressing itself as beauty, truth, goodness, and especially love! . . . Creation is lit up with the numinous. —Numinous: that's God saying Hi! [smiling again]

"And *faith* is the surrender to this great gift of love, Life! . . . to be alive in Creation. . . . Submit to it — not in the sense of passive resignation, but in acceptance and participation in being!

"I give up . . .Take me. — you say in prayer. . . .You give back, in sacrifice, what was never yours.

"So, you see, it's something like this . . . to use an image or a metaphor. —After all, I'm a poet of sorts . . . not a philosopher or theologian, eh?

"In total inhalation, in the act of Eucharist, you eat the Mystical Body, the Cosmic Christ, by accepting, by participating, in joy, the total charity of your being in creation! —The I of you dies to One! . . . You are, in the truest sense, what you eat.

"And in total exhalation you offer up, give back, go home in *redemption*. . . . You do this by curing the inner split between you and God (the Incarnate Creator) — this division, what we often-times call Original Sin in mystical theology.

"That's why you go to the monastery, the primary reason any-way. It's to do that — to heal the illusion of separation . . . the sepa-ration of you from your true person, from the world in creation, and especially from God.

"You see —It's all . . . we're all One!

"So relax. Quit apologizing.

"God loves you or you wouldn't be . . . eh? [laughing]

"Sure."

We arrived at the airport a few minutes before seven. I pulled up in front of the passenger departure gate, dropped Tom off with the luggage, gave him directions to the restaurant, and parked the car.

When I walked in, Tom was sitting at the counter, reading aloud the menu to the waitress as if it were a dramatic poem, both of them laughing. He was feeling good, hungry, and had already ordered a big breakfast.

"Lots of great stuff here, Ron. Especially the second stanza in bold type. Free verse, so what'll you have?" he asked in a generous voice, rubbing his palms together.

"I'm a minimilist. Just a cup of coffee'll do it," I said. "This is my early period," sliding onto the stool beside him.

"Ooops!" looking at his watch. "Time to read my secular office."

Tom hurried out the door to the newstand and was back with a copy of the *New Yorker* just as his food was being served. He placed the open magazine on the counter beside his plate and turned the pages while he ate.

"My favorite reading," he looked up, smiling. "All kinds of strange found poems in here."

True. That's where Tom got so much material, the advertising slogans especially, to insert in his collection, *Cables to the Ace* — the manuscript I so arrogantly refused to type at the time because I thought much of the material "sloppy and not good enough" compared to his earlier work (again, always at least five years behind in understanding what he was about in his poetry).

Now, the check paid, a dollar tip left proudly on the counter, the tote bag swinging at his side as he took long strides —"Don't want to waste any time," over his shoulder—we found the right gate.

Tom was first in line.

"Want to get a seat by the window so I can see everything," he grinned.

Eye of the poet, always, I thought. Wants to sky-view the landscape calligraphy as he passes over the huge bulge and roll of the continent westward. Develop the photo-images later in his pocket journal.

And with Tom becoming anxious to get up and away and on with it . . . I just stood there awkwardly beside him, out of words. *Goodbye, have a nice trip* — swallowed silent a last time.

Then, involuntarily, without thinking, I repeated what I had said the night before, "You won't be coming back. . . . You'll stay over there." —Still playful, but (with unwanted intimations), it came out more serious.

Tom just smiled. "Naw, I'll be back. Can't get rid of me that easily." Then, looking me straight in the eye a caught moment, "Anyway, the Abbot wouldn't allow that now, would he?"

Silent, holding the lock of his look as long as possible, I dropped my head and reached out and shook his hand a last time. *So long Tom.*

Suddenly, I was weary. I felt exhausted and spent. There was nothing more to be done. I wouldn't wait to see the plane off.

Tom was still standing there in line as I turned and walked away — *don't look back* — on out the door and to my car.

And that was the end of it. The last time I would ever see and be with Tom Merton.

———————◆———————

The sound of the monastery bell awakens me from my stare out over the dimming bottomlands. My shoulder aches from leaning against the wood porchpost.

The second bell now as I straighten to stand, reaching down into the side pocket of my jacket.

Author on the porch of Merton's hermitage.

Here, clear on the air, the third bell . . . and the notebook in my hand, opened to the fourth bell ringing its echo against the blank page with my pen printing words to the fifth bell sounding a long fade to silence and my hand held still, slowing, beneath

> a long and low sky
> narrowing into sunset—
> the five o'clock bells

moving my lips as I stoop and lay the open notebook on the smooth concrete floor of the hermitage porch.

Standing, I reach into my other jacket pocket for the page torn from the notebook earlier, then walk over to the door and pin the paper onto the small nail about eye-level in the wood there: a farewell message to Tom, from Tom . . . using the name (among others) we shared and sometimes called each other—

> I am Hsu Yu
> I am old and alone
> My ears are clean
> Tell me nothing

"What, I hope, Tom, you would have said to anyone visiting here — if you had known then, as I do now. . . that you would never again return to this place," I say aloud as the wind lifts the edge of the white sheet and laps it against the door.

"Or better yet — let the wind blow all words away."

The sound of my voice good to hear after so long a silence. But gone again . . . just the faint *th tick* and

> a sudden shiver
> hearing the wind blow dead leaves
> across his workboots

as I turn around to the sun already dropped behind the trees lining the far hills in a black brush of branchtops blooming the horizon an orange aura of light — late afternoon.

Now the moon, and . . . the bells of *Vespers* will be ringing soon. Have to hurry . . . Ready? (looking around one last time) . . . Got everything?

There — my notebook . . . lying on the porch, waiting

> a December moon
> to write *scarecrow* on the page
> now covered with leaves

shaking in the wind, now still, as I walk over, stoop, and

> to the dry brown leaf
> with a fingertip just touch
> —how cold the stem cracks!

A final haiku homage, to Tom . . . as I place my right knee to the cold concrete and bow my head to the tall wooden cross signed high to heaven his hermitage home.

A genuflection . . . a benediction . . . in his memory.

Unwanted, unwelcome (I know), but—

The hermitage is behind me now. I am walking down the clear stretch of pasture grass covered with snow, and I do not look back because nothing more is there for me. I can see the

*View of monastery from road that winds through woods
to Merton's hermitage.*

monastery church about a mile away across the valley, and that is where I am heading. Not to the church, but the monks' cemetery alongside and behind it. *There* is the last place to visit — Tom's grave.

And walking towards that place, the final destination of this pilgrim path, what I have been putting off all day — the details of that fateful event now twenty years ago begin coming back. My memory again open to. . . .

A bell ringing. Closer. A second bell sounding full upon the first, and a third gathering both echoes in a closed descent clearing the air and my head to hear

> Ah Issho
> Soon I too
> Will be old
>
> Will death
> (when it comes)
> Bring from the west
> A cloud of snow
> For me as well

—calling Tom by yet another of our names . . . my words emptying the long buried lament already voiced inside me as I open the small iron gate of the enclosure wall and enter the large area next to the new guesthouse.

The Stations of the Cross stand one by one along a worn path making a circle at the bottom of a slight slope to the left.

I do not go that way, but keep walking straight until I stand alongside the high white stucco church, near and almost beneath the reaching limbs of a thin cedar tree. At my feet, a small iron cross painted white.

Leaning close to the bronze plate on the marker, my eyes move along the raised letters shining its inscription

---

FR. LOUIS MERTON
DIED DEC. 10, 1968

—the sunken signature of good Brother Lou-ie . . . Thomas Merton.

Bending closer now, my right hand grips an arm of the cross and, again feeling the cold come off the metal into my palm, I let the words of this vision print its epitaph in my memory—

> a cold wind
> freezing to crust
> the snow
> already
> going gray
> slowly
> to darkness
> on white ice
> I stand
> with closed
> eyes
> dreaming
> deep
> a float
> into bare
> black
> branches fading
> out
> to this

—then raise my eyes to the wide darkening sky, and again ask myself why I am here. . . . Why did I return to this grave place?

But the clear winter air answers only with a lone bird circling high and black above the Trappist Cemetery, its ascension winged signature sliding silently over the rows of white crosses slanting away down the hill.

> YOU'RE HERE TO REMEMBER, TO REMIND OTHERS WHO MIGHT HAVE FORGOTTEN. TO TELL THE MANY WHO KNOW LITTLE, AND THE MORE WHO HAVE NEVER EVEN HEARD HIS NAME — WHAT IT IS YOU HAVE TO SAY ABOUT THIS MAN . . . THOMAS MERTON.

Suddenly this inner voice is silenced by the sound of bells! . . .
their windy cold echoes fading the light, gathering the night, folding in with gray the whole stone structure of the Abbey Church,
choiring the clouds with their Trappist tolls:

Vespers.

The time of his burial.

The same bells. —This time falling slowly, sinking softly into
the snow-covered grave grass.

Tom.

Once again, as long ago, left alone. Lying deep in the dark earth
of his first and final home.

Gethsemani.

*Iron cross gravemarker
of Fr. Louis Merton in
monk's cemetery at
Abbey of Gethsemani.*

December 10, 1988

now too   outside this cell

the zero dawn air breathes
its hushed signature through stone

a porous prayer emptying white
my window with praise

the gift glow touch:
Presence

    It is morning now, and I am back home where I began this trip along the songline. Time to call a halt. A farewell, and nothing more to add.

    Tom Merton is gone. And I'm left with the 'reminders'.

    On a hook, at the foot of the stairs, hangs his old jacket. On the mantel, in the livingroom, are stacked his books and jazz records. And in a box, here on the desk beside me, his letters. . . . About all that's left of those good days together, here now recalled. —Except for the big black western hat that Tom gave me that last day, and

which (silly gesture, always the fool) I pushed tight onto my head to come down to this small room, my writing place, to begin again, and end, this Memory Vision.

But Tom Merton gave me much more than all of this, these words here. And that's what I'd like to pass along to my wife and children, my friends . . . and anyone else interested.

To be sure, Tom always knew me much better than I did him (as was the case with most whom he touched). And many times, Tom was telling himself (moreso than me) much of what he had to say about life and the "heartbreaking beauty and joy of it."

So, enough said about Merton the philosopher, Merton the theologian, Merton the whatever. The entire story of all that more than already told in the many books books books. . . .

My *say* here is no more than a remembrance portrait. A Thank

The 'road back' — from the hermitage sans adieu.

You! of sorts. —What I'm after in these few words is the spiritual seed that Tom planted in my person . . . the *presence* that I shared in those too-brief years we passed-thru together.

And well I know how Tom would smile at much of this now — the way I, and so many others, misinterpreted his vocation: romantically. . . . Because that's not at all what he meant in his writings and work, in his life.

But, just as he, once — we were impressionable young men who sought the monastic haven and heaven of silence and solitude . . . contemplation.

To sink into the dusk-breathing stones of old Abbey walls. To find the spiritual cell where. . . .

And what I still long for sometimes now, these many years later. —A man growing old. A monk in exile . . . missing home.

The man of Tao
Remains unknown
Perfect virtue
Produces nothing
'No-Self'
Is 'True-Self'
And the greatest man
Is Nobody

THOMAS MERTON
from
The Way of Chuang Tzu

Name Index

About the Author

Author at Monks Pond.

A CLOSE PERSONAL FRIEND OF THOMAS MERTON and a prolific poet, RON SEITZ was instrumental in founding the Thomas Merton Studies Center at Bellarmine College. His poetry has appeared in a wide variety of periodicals, including *Monks Pond, Commonweal, Green River Review, West Coast Review, America, U.S. Catholic,* and *Approaches.* He travels regularly conducting poetry readings and speaking about the life and work of Thomas Merton. In addition, he is a featured lecturer at the Third International Merton Conference, in Colorado Springs, to commemorate the twenty-fifth anniversary of Merton's death in 1968. His prose articles have been published in such magazines as *U.S. Catholic, St. Anthony Messenger, Way, Twigs, The Courier-Journal Magazine,* and *Kentucky Poetry Review.*

Seitz holds a Master's degree from the University of Louisville and has over twenty-six years of college-level teaching experience, which includes courses in creative writing, literature, religious studies, and the humanities. In addition to several television interviews, he also appeared on National Public Radio in a documentary/interview entitled "Thomas Merton: The Least and the Last Men." He is recipient of the Catholic Press Association's Journalism Award for Best Short Story (entitled "Once Upon a Church") that appeared in *U.S. Catholic/Jubilee.*

Seitz's professional memberships include the Mary Anderson Center for the Arts at Mount St. Francis, Indiana, and the Abbey Center for the Study of Ethics and Culture at the Abbey of Gethsemani in Trappist, Kentucky.

Married and father of three grown children, Ron Seitz currently resides in Louisville, Kentucky. His publications include several volumes of poetry. This is his first full-length book. He describes SONG FOR NOBODY as "a synthesis of shared experience, correspondence, and intellectual/artistic expression of two poets' spiritual journey . . . using the novelistic, fictional technique of characterization and dialogue." It was the author's design to present Thomas Merton "in the flesh, concretely, dramatically, experientially," as opposed to the treatment of a critical biography. "Ideally," he concludes, "the book presents Merton as a 'living presence', a palpable person (in all of his earthly humanness), a man of intelligence, humor, creativity, wisdom, spirituality, and *warmth* — one who *enjoys* people, beauty, nature, the entire eucharistic sacrament of creation."

Seitz believes, "This book is a song for nobody . . . but for *every Spirit!*"